What I Eat So My Body Doesn't Quit: A Sassy Kitchen Rescue Plan for Your Gut, Skin, Joints, and Sanity

ANDREA D. RATLIFF

What I Eat So My Body Doesn't Quit: A Sassy Kitchen Rescue Plan for Your Gut, Skin, Joints, and Sanity

ANDREA D. RATLIFF

© 2025 by Andrea Ratliff.

All rights reserved. No part of this publication may be reproduced, distributed, or transmitted in any form or by any means, including photocopying, recording, or other electronic or mechanical methods, without the prior written permission of the publisher, except in the case of brief quotations embodied in critical reviews and certain other noncommercial uses permitted by copyright law.

CONTENTS

Preface

1 Introduction to Anti-Inflammatory Lifestyle and Its Significance 7

BREAKFAST 26

LUNCH 37

SOUPS AND STEWS 48

SALADS AND DRESSINGS 59

MAIN DISHES 71

SIDE DISHES 89

SNACKS 101

DESSERTS 112

BEVERAGES 123

SAUCES, DIPS, AND CONDIMENTS 134

    SYMPTOMS/FLARE UP JOURNAL 143

ANDREA D. RATLIFF

PREFACE

Let's be real for a second: If you're holding this book, chances are you're feeling something. Maybe it's the kind of joint pain that makes getting out of bed feel like a group project. Or maybe your gut's been staging a silent protest (or a very loud one). Maybe you're living in a fog, snapping at people you love, and wondering when normal stopped feeling like an option.

I see you—because I've been you. And I finally got tired of the guessing, the Googling, the guilt, and the gas (yeah, I said it). That's when I started to discover the quiet but powerful force behind it all: inflammation.

Here's the kicker: chronic inflammation is now known to be the root of nearly every major health issue we're facing today. We're talking heart disease, diabetes, autoimmune flares, brain fog, fatigue, anxiety, and even skin problems like acne and eczema. According to the World Health Organization, non-communicable diseases (many linked to chronic inflammation) account for nearly 74% of all deaths globally. And guess what's fanning the flames? The modern lifestyle—hello, ultra-processed snacks, stress spirals, sleep struggles, and sedentary days.

But here's the part that lit a fire under me (and not the bad kind): you can fight inflammation every single day—right from your kitchen. That's what this book is all about. No starvation. No shame. No cardboard "health" food. Just real, delicious meals that love you back.

What I Eat So My Body Doesn't Quit is the sassy survival guide I wish I had when I was trying to figure out why I felt 82 at 35. It's for anyone who wants to take back their energy, soothe their joints, flatten the bloat, sharpen their mind, and glow from the inside out—without losing their mind in the process.

This isn't a diet. It's a rescue plan. One bite at a time, we're calming the chaos and giving our bodies what they've been begging for.

So grab your fork, turn up your sass, and let's get you back to feeling like you.

We're not here to be perfect—we're here to feel better. Let's cook like we mean it.

PART ONE
Introduction to Anti-Inflammatory Lifestyle and Its Significance

1. Hey, What's Inflammation Anyway?

Alright, let's kick things off with a word that sounds a little science-y but is actually super important when it comes to how you feel every day: inflammation.

You've probably heard it tossed around on health shows, blogs, or in those wellness articles that tell you to "fight inflammation with food." But if you're anything like I was in the beginning, you might be thinking—Okay, but what does that actually mean?

So, here's the scoop.

Inflammation is your body's built-in alarm system. It's not a bad thing, at least not at first. Imagine you step on a tack (ouch!). Almost immediately, your immune system sends out the troops—white blood cells, chemicals, all the good guys—to the injury site to help you heal. You might get redness, swelling, maybe even a little pain. That's your body doing its job, saying:

"Hey, something's wrong here—let's fix it."

That kind of inflammation? Totally normal. It's called acute inflammation, and it usually comes and goes as needed. Like a helpful firefighter who shows up, puts out the flames, and heads back to the station.

But here's where things can go sideways. Sometimes, the alarm doesn't turn off. Your body keeps sending out those fire trucks even though there's no fire. That's what we call chronic inflammation, and unlike the short-term kind, this one doesn't come with flashing lights and obvious symptoms. It's sneaky.

Instead of helping you heal, chronic inflammation quietly simmers in the background. Over time, it starts to wear you down. You might not even realize it's happening—you just know you feel "off."

Maybe it's...

- That stubborn brain fog that makes you forget what you walked into the room for.
- Achy joints even though you haven't done anything strenuous.
- Digestive issues that seem to pop up out of nowhere.
- Or maybe it's just plain exhaustion that lingers no matter how much you sleep.

I like to compare it to a smoke alarm that won't stop beeping, even when there's no smoke. It's annoying, sure—but if you ignore it long enough, it could mean trouble.

So, what causes this kind of inflammation to hang around?

Things like stress, lack of sleep, too much sugar, processed foods, sitting too much, and even loneliness (yep, that's a big one) can keep your body in "red alert" mode. And when that happens day after day, year after year, it can start damaging healthy tissues and organs. That's when chronic diseases like arthritis, heart disease, diabetes, and even depression can creep in.

But here's the good news—and this is the part I love sharing: You're not stuck with it.

There are things you can do every single day to cool the fire, gently turn off the alarm, and help your body settle into a state of calm.

And guess what?
It starts with what you put on your plate.
(It also involves how you move, rest, and manage stress—but we'll get to all of that.)

So if you've been feeling tired, achy, puffy, or just not quite like yourself lately, inflammation could be part of the puzzle. But don't worry—this isn't about rules and restrictions. It's about adding in foods and habits that love you back.

2. What Can Set Off Chronic Inflammation?

Okay, now that we've talked about what inflammation is, let's get into what can actually trigger it—and keep it hanging around like an uninvited houseguest who just won't leave.

Because here's the deal: chronic inflammation doesn't show up out of nowhere. It's often the result of everyday habits that quietly pile up over time. And no, this isn't about blame or guilt—life happens. But when we understand what's stirring the pot, we can start making changes that really stick.

So, let's break it down.

Processed Junk Food (Yep, Those Chips and Sodas)

You knew this one was coming, right?

I'm not here to food-shame anyone—we've all had our moments with a bag of chips and a soda (hello, road trips and stressful Tuesdays). But here's the truth: processed foods are one of the biggest drivers of chronic inflammation.

They're often loaded with:

- Added sugars (sneaky little things hiding in everything)
- Refined carbs (think white bread, crackers, cookies)
- Unhealthy fats (like trans fats and too many omega-6 oils)

All of that can overload your system and keep your immune response on high alert. It's like fueling a fire with lighter fluid instead of water. No wonder your body's inflamed!

Sitting Around Too Much

Ever heard the phrase, "sitting is the new smoking"?

Dramatic, but not totally wrong. Our bodies are meant to move, stretch, and get the blood flowing. When we sit for long periods (hello, desk jobs, binge-watching marathons, or endless scrolling), our circulation slows down, our muscles stiffen, and yep—inflammation can sneak in.

The fix doesn't have to be intense. You don't need to run marathons. Even short walks, gentle stretches, or dancing in your kitchen to your favorite playlist can work wonders.

Constant Stress (Been There)

This one hits close to home, right?

We all deal with stress—it's part of being human. But when it becomes chronic—like deadlines, financial worry, family drama, or just never feeling like you can exhale—it can throw your whole system off.

Your body doesn't know the difference between being chased by a tiger and just stressing over emails. It reacts the same way—by releasing cortisol and other stress hormones. And if that stress switch stays "on" all the time, inflammation tags along for the ride.

Not Enough Sleep

Raise your hand if you've ever told yourself "just one more episode"... and then suddenly it's 2 a.m.
Guilty as charged. But the thing is, sleep is when your body heals. It's not just rest—it's repair. If you're skimping on sleep (even just a few nights a week), your body never fully gets to do its overnight housekeeping. The result? You guessed it—inflammation.

Even 7–9 solid hours a night can make a huge difference in how you feel, think, digest, and recover.

A Cranky Gut

Your gut is more than just where digestion happens—it's home to trillions of bacteria that impact everything from your immune system to your mood. When those bacteria are out of balance (thanks to antibiotics, stress, poor diet, or lack of fiber), it can create a leaky gut situation. That means tiny particles slip into your bloodstream where they don't belong, and your immune system gets triggered... again and again.

Keeping your gut happy = a calmer, less inflamed body. (Don't worry—we'll get into how to feed those gut bugs soon.)

Basically... Life Out of Balance

Let's be real. Sometimes, it's not just one thing—it's all of the above, swirling together. Life gets busy. We stay up late, eat convenience food, skip movement, get stuck in stress cycles, and forget to check in with ourselves.

The good news? Every small change helps. This isn't about being perfect. It's about creating a little more balance—one meal, one walk, one deep breath at a time.

Because when you start dialing down the things that fuel inflammation, your body notices. It starts to relax, repair, and reset.

And trust me—you'll feel the difference.

3. So What's an Anti-Inflammatory Diet Really?

Let's take a deep breath and talk about the part everyone's curious about: the food.
Because when you hear anti-inflammatory diet," it might sound like one of those trendy, hard-to-follow programs that expects you to toss everything in your pantry, give up joy, and survive on kale and lemon water.

But let me stop you right there. This is not one of those all-or-nothing, guilt-heavy plans. There are no weird powders, no starvation, and no "perfect" required.

The anti-inflammatory way of eating is more like a loving reset button. It's about feeding your body in a way that helps it chill out—to lower the internal noise, reduce the stress signals, and help your cells get back to what they're supposed to be doing: healing, energizing, protecting, and supporting you.

So, What Does It Actually Look Like?

Picture this...

Your plate is full of vibrant colors—deep greens, bright reds, juicy oranges, and maybe even some purples. There's some healthy fat drizzled on top (hello, olive oil), maybe a piece of grilled salmon or roasted chickpeas, and something fermented like a scoop of sauerkraut or a spoonful of tangy yogurt. There's texture, flavor, and satisfaction.

That's the vibe of an anti-inflammatory meal. It's not about eating "rabbit food." It's about eating real food—food that's been grown, caught, raised, or prepared with as little processing as possible.

It's also about tuning in to your body and giving it what it actually wants and needs—like a long, soothing exhale after a stressful day. You're saying, "Hey body, I see you. I've got you."

Why Does It Work?

Here's the cool part: the foods that calm inflammation aren't magic potions—they're full of things your body recognizes and knows how to use.

- Antioxidants that fight off stress and damage.
- Healthy fats that soothe your cells.
- Fiber that feeds your gut and keeps things moving.
- Vitamins and minerals that support your immune system.
- Natural compounds (like those found in turmeric, berries, and leafy greens) that act like peacekeepers inside you.

When you eat this way consistently—again, not perfectly—you're helping your body lower its defenses. You're telling your immune system, "It's safe to stand down."

And that's when healing really starts.

It's Not About Perfection—It's About Progress

Let me be super clear here: you don't have to get it all right on day one. You don't have to give up your favorite comfort food forever, or buy all organic everything, or meal prep every Sunday (unless you want to!).

What matters most is the direction you're heading. If you're swapping sugary cereal for oatmeal and berries a few times a week, that's a win. If you're adding a handful of spinach to your smoothie or choosing olive oil over butter for your stir-fry, you're doing it. Those little changes build up—and your body notices.

The anti-inflammatory way of eating isn't about restriction—it's about restoration. It's about giving your body what it's been craving all along: real nourishment, less stress, and a little room to breathe.

So, ready to see which foods actually help your body feel its best?

4. The Feel-Good Foods (a.k.a. Your Anti-Inflammatory Friends)

Now for the fun part—what you can eat. Because let's be honest, most "diets" start with a long list of things you have to cut out. This? This is about what you can pile onto your plate to help your body feel strong, calm, and energized.

These are the foods that work with your body, not against it. They don't cause chaos—they help clean it up. They bring down the noise, cool the internal fire, and make your cells do a little happy dance.

Let's meet your inflammation-fighting dream team:

Healthy Fats

Let's start with the all-stars: omega-3s

These are the kinds of fats your body loves—the kind that help reduce inflammation, support your brain, and even keep your joints feeling smooth and steady.

- Salmon, sardines, mackerel – Fatty fish are some of the best sources of omega-3s out there. Try for a few servings a week if you can.
- Walnuts, chia seeds, flaxseeds – These plant-based gems are perfect for topping oatmeal, tossing into smoothies, or sprinkling over salads.
- Olive oil – Drizzle it, dip into it, and cook with it. Extra virgin olive oil is like a soothing balm for your cells—seriously, it's that good.

Think of healthy fats as your body's built-in firefighters. They're here to help cool things down.

Colorful Fruits & Veggies

If it grows from the ground and has a vibrant color, chances are it's packed with antioxidants—those little warriors that fight off stress and inflammation.

- Berries – Blueberries, raspberries, strawberries… all loaded with fiber and brain-boosting benefits.
- Leafy greens – Spinach, kale, arugula—these guys are full of vitamins and minerals your body uses to heal.
- Bell peppers, carrots, beets, broccoli, red cabbage – The more color variety on your plate, the better. Nature didn't give them those bright shades for nothing!

Pro tip: Try to "eat the rainbow" every day. It's fun, it's beautiful, and your body will thank you.

Whole Grains

Say goodbye to ultra-refined white stuff and hello to grains that still know who they are.

- Oats, brown rice, quinoa, barley, farro – These are complex carbs that your body can actually use for energy without spiking your blood sugar.
- They're rich in fiber, which helps keep your digestion smooth and your gut microbes well-fed.

Your gut loves fiber—and a happy gut means less inflammation.

Spices & Herbs

Let's talk flavor and healing. Some of the most powerful anti-inflammatory tools are already sitting in your spice rack.

- Turmeric – This bright yellow spice is famous for a reason. It contains curcumin, a compound that helps fight inflammation big time. Just make sure to pair it with black pepper—it boosts absorption by up to 2,000%!
- Ginger – Fresh, powdered, or in tea—it's warming, soothing, and great for digestion too.
- Garlic – Beyond making everything taste better, it has compounds that support the immune system and reduce inflammation.

Your kitchen can double as your medicine cabinet. Pretty cool, right?

Gut-Boosters

You've heard me say it before: your gut is your second brain. When it's happy, everything else—from your mood to your immune system—tends to fall into place.

- Probiotic foods – Think yogurt with live cultures, kefir, sauerkraut, kimchi, and miso. These help populate your gut with the good bacteria that keep inflammation in check
- Prebiotics – These are the foods that feed your good bugs. Bananas, asparagus, onions, garlic, leeks—they all help create a thriving gut garden.

Gut health = whole-body health. Don't underestimate those little microbes!

Little Treats That Do Good

Yes, friends—there's room for treats. And not just the boring "healthy" kind either.

- Dark chocolate – Look for 70% cacao or higher. A square or two is rich in antioxidants and totally satisfying.
- Coffee and green tea – Full of anti-inflammatory compounds (in moderation, of course). Sip and smile.

This isn't about deprivation—it's about upgrading your treats.

So there you have it: a pantry full of delicious, satisfying, healing foods that love you back.

Start adding them in, a little at a time. Swap a soda for green tea. Toss some blueberries into your oatmeal. Drizzle olive oil over roasted veggies.

These small, joyful steps? They add up fast.

5. The Inflammation Instigators (Time to Break Up with These)

Alright, now that we've celebrated all the delicious, healing foods you can load up on, it's time to talk about the ones that... well, stir the pot a little too much.

These are the foods that can keep your body's alarm system stuck in the "on" position. And when you eat them all the time (like so many of us have without even realizing it), they can quietly add fuel to the inflammation fire.

But let me be super clear about something:

This isn't about perfection. You don't have to toss everything in your pantry or feel guilty for enjoying a cookie or a slice of pizza. Life's too short for that kind of stress—and stress is inflammatory too!

The goal here is awareness. When you know which foods tend to cause trouble, you can start making choices that lean more toward healing and less toward harm.

Let's take a look at the usual suspects:

Added Sugars (In Pretty Much Everything Processed)

Sugar is sneaky—it shows up in sauces, salad dressings, breads, "healthy" granola bars, and even soups. The problem is that excess sugar spikes your blood sugar, then drops it fast, which stresses your system. Over time, this up-and-down roller coaster leads to—you guessed it—chronic inflammation.

And it's not just about candy and desserts. Look out for:

- Corn syrup
- Cane sugar
- Dextrose, fructose, glucose (anything ending in -ose)
- "Natural" sweeteners in disguise

Tip: Start checking labels. Even cutting back a little can have a big impact on your energy, mood, and joint pain.

White Carbs (Bye White Bread and Muffins)

Refined carbs are stripped of their nutrients and fiber, which means they behave a lot like sugar in your body— fast, dramatic, and not in a good way.

We're talking:

- White bread
- Regular pasta
- White rice
- Pastries and muffins

They spike blood sugar, throw off your gut, and offer zero lasting fuel.

Swap in: whole grains like quinoa, oats, brown rice, or even cauliflower rice when you're in the mood to mix things up.

Processed Meats (We're Looking at You, Bacon and Hot Dogs)

As tasty as bacon might be on a Sunday morning, processed meats are some of the most inflammatory foods out there.

They often contain:

- Preservatives
- Additives like nitrates
- Excess sodium and saturated fat

These ingredients have been linked to higher levels of inflammation and an increased risk of heart disease and certain cancers. Not fun.

It's not "never," it's just... "not every day." Think of bacon and deli meats as more of an occasional indulgence than an everyday staple.

Trans Fats (Sneaky Little Things)

Trans fats are the ultimate troublemakers. They mess with your heart, your brain, and yep—your inflammation levels.

You'll find them in:

- Packaged baked goods
- Some fried foods
- Margarine or shortening
- Non-dairy coffee creamers

Even though they've been banned in many places, small amounts still sneak into processed snacks. So again—check those labels. Look for "partially hydrogenated oils" and steer clear.

Too Much Corn or Soybean Oil

Now, a little corn or soybean oil isn't the end of the world. But when they're your go-to oils for cooking or show up in everything you eat, it can tip the balance.

These oils are super high in omega-6 fatty acids. And while your body does need some omega-6, too much (and not enough omega-3) can keep inflammation simmering.

Try this instead: Olive oil, avocado oil, or coconut oil for cooking. You'll still get great flavor, minus the inflammatory side effects.

The Big Picture: It's About the Pattern, Not Perfection

Let's be real. You're not going to quit sugar, carbs, and bacon overnight—and you don't have to. This is about what you eat most of the time, not what you eat once in a while. The occasional treat is part of a joyful, balanced life.

So instead of focusing on restriction, shift your energy toward crowding in the good stuff. Fill your plate with healing foods, and you'll naturally start to crowd out the ones that aren't serving you.

And every time you choose something that supports your body's healing? That's a win.

6. It's Not Just Food—Lifestyle Matters Too

Okay, so we've covered what's going on inside your fridge and pantry—but what's going on in your everyday life matters just as much when it comes to inflammation.

Food is a huge part of the puzzle, but it's not the only piece. Your movement, your sleep, your stress levels, and even how often you laugh (seriously!) can either help your body stay calm or keep it in a constant state of stress.

But don't panic—this isn't about becoming a yoga-practicing, meal-prepping, early-rising superhuman overnight. It's about little shifts in your day that support your body instead of working against it.

Let's break it down:

Move That Body

You don't need a gym membership or a 90-minute workout.
Even a simple daily walk can be incredibly anti-inflammatory.

Why? Because movement:

- Boosts circulation
- Reduces stress
- Helps your lymphatic system flush out toxins
- Supports your joints and muscles

The goal is to move your body in a way that feels good—whether that's dancing in your kitchen, stretching in the morning, or walking your dog after dinner.

It doesn't have to be fancy. It just has to be consistent.

Chill Out (Seriously)

Stress is one of the sneakiest inflammation triggers out there. And not just big, dramatic stress—daily low-level stress (hello, traffic, emails, deadlines, and family chaos) can slowly wear you down and keep your body in fight-or-flight mode.

Here's the magic: even just a few minutes of calm can make a huge difference.

- Try deep breathing (inhale for 4, exhale for 6)
- Listen to calming music
- Try meditation or prayer

- Take a few phone-free minutes in the sun
- Journal or doodle
- Laugh (really—it's therapy)

Stress management isn't a luxury—it's medicine.

Sleep Is Medicine

Want to reduce inflammation without lifting a finger?

Go to bed. Seriously.

When you sleep, your body shifts into repair mode. It heals tissues, balances hormones, and regulates your immune response.

Most adults need 7–9 hours—and yes, the quality of your sleep matters just as much as the quantity.

If sleep is a struggle:

- Create a relaxing bedtime routine
- Cut screen time an hour before bed
- Keep your bedroom cool and dark
- Try magnesium or herbal tea (like chamomile or valerian root)

Better sleep = less inflammation = more energy, clarity, and healing.

Love Your Gut

We've touched on this already, but it's worth repeating: Your gut health is deeply connected to your inflammation levels.

Your gut houses around 70% of your immune system—so keeping it in balance is key.

That means:

- Feeding it probiotics (like yogurt, kefir, sauerkraut)
- Supporting it with prebiotics (bananas, garlic, onions, oats)
- Drinking plenty of water
- Managing stress (yep, stress affects your gut too
- Avoiding unnecessary antibiotics

A happy gut means better digestion, more energy, clearer skin, and fewer flare-ups. It's kind of a big deal.

Cook More at Home

I get it—takeout is easy. But when you cook at home—even just a few times a week—you have way more control over what goes into your body.

No hidden sugars, no sketchy oils, no mystery ingredients.

Start simple:

- Roast a sheet pan of veggies
- Cook a pot of soup or chili
- Try overnight oats for breakfast
- Keep olive oil, lemon, garlic, and herbs on hand—they make everything taste better

Homemade doesn't mean hard. It means you're showing your body some love with every bite.

Here's the bottom line: Healing inflammation isn't just about food. It's about creating a lifestyle that makes your body feel safe, supported, and strong.

You don't need to overhaul everything overnight. Just pick one small habit to start with.
Go for a walk. Make a home-cooked meal. Breathe deeply for a few minutes. Get to bed 30 minutes earlier.

Each one of those is a step toward healing. And before you know it, those small changes add up to a body—and life—that feels a whole lot better.

7. Real-Life Tips to Get Started (Because Overwhelm Is Real)

Look, we've covered a lot—foods to eat, foods to limit, lifestyle tweaks, gut health, stress, sleep, movement... Phew!

If your brain is spinning right now, just know: you're not alone.

When you're trying to feel better, it's easy to fall into the "I need to do everything perfectly right now" trap. But that kind of thinking? It's the fast track to burnout.

So instead of trying to overhaul your entire life in one week, let's talk about a few real-life, low-stress ways to get the ball rolling.

Because small, doable changes add up fast—and they stick.

Swap Sugary Cereal for Oatmeal with Berries

Breakfast doesn't have to be complicated. Just ditch the boxed cereal (loaded with sugar and not much else) and go for something that fuels you and fights inflammation.

Try:

- Rolled or steel-cut oat

- Toss in some frozen or fresh berries
- Sprinkle with flaxseeds or walnuts
- Add cinnamon or a drizzle of honey if you want

Boom: fiber, antioxidants, healthy fats, and steady energy.

Craving Chips? Try Roasted Chickpeas or Nuts

You don't have to give up crunchy, salty snacks—you just have to swap them for ones that actually support your health.

Roasted chickpeas are shockingly satisfying. Toss them with olive oil, a little salt, and your favorite spices, then roast until crispy.

Or go for a handful of:

- Almonds
- Cashews
- Pistachios
- Walnuts

Pro tip: Keep portion sizes reasonable, especially with nuts—they're nutrient-dense, but easy to over-snack on.

Keep Frozen Veggies on Hand for Quick Dinners

Frozen veggies are a lifesaver on busy nights. They're picked at peak ripeness and flash-frozen, so you still get lots of nutrients—plus, no chopping!

Toss them in a stir fry, soup, pasta, or roast them straight from frozen with a little olive oil and garlic powder.

Keep things like:

- Broccoli
- Cauliflower
- Spinach
- Mixed peppers
- Edamame

Dinner doesn't have to be gourmet—it just has to nourish you.

Make a Big Batch of Soup or Grain Bowls for Easy Lunches

Meal prep sounds fancy, but it's really just about making your life easier. Take one hour on the weekend, and your future self will thank you all week.

Ideas:

- Lentil or veggie-packed soup
- Quinoa with roasted veggies, chickpeas, and a drizzle of tahini or pesto
- Brown rice bowls with greens, avocado, and grilled salmon or tofu

Portion it out, pop it in the fridge, and you've got anti-inflammatory power meals ready to go.

Treat Yourself to Some High-Quality Dark Chocolate

Let's end on a high note, shall we?

Yes—you can have chocolate. And not just as a cheat, but as a legit anti-inflammatory treat (when it's the good kind).

Look for:

- At least 70% cacao
- Minimal added sugar
- Organic or fair-trade if possible

Pair a square with your tea or have it as an after-dinner treat. You're still nourishing yourself—and enjoying life while you do it.

One Step at a Time, Friend

Remember, this journey isn't about rules—it's about relief. It's about feeling better in your own body, one simple swap, one walk, one breath, one veggie-packed meal at a time.

You don't need to do it perfectly. You just need to begin.

And you already have.

ANDREA D. RATLIFF

4-week Anti-inflammatory Meal Plan

Week 1

Monday
- Breakfast: Oatmeal with Berries and Walnuts (p.22)
- Lunch: Grilled Salmon Salad with Olive Oil Vinaigrette (p.33)
- Dinner: Baked Salmon with Lemon and Dill (p.67)
- Snack: Apple Slices with Almond Butter (p.98)

Tuesday
- Breakfast: Greek Yogurt with Chia Seeds and Strawberries (p.23)
- Lunch: Lentil and Vegetable Soup with Turmeric (p.34)
- Dinner: Chickpea and Spinach Coconut Curry (p.68)
- Snack: Roasted Chickpeas with Sea Salt and Paprika (p.104)

Wednesday
- Breakfast: Smoothie with Spinach, Blueberries, Banana, and Flaxseeds (p.25)
- Lunch: Sardine and Avocado Wrap (p.36)
- Dinner: Sweet Potato and Black Bean Tacos (p.70)
- Snack: Chia Seed Pudding with Berries and Cinnamon (p.109)

Thursday
- Breakfast: Avocado Toast on Whole Grain Bread (p.24)
- Lunch: Quinoa Bowl with Roasted Veggies and Tahini Dressing (p.35)
- Dinner: Zucchini Noodles with Pesto and Cherry Tomatoes (p.72)
- Snack: Fresh Berries with a Handful of Walnuts (p.97)

Friday
- Breakfast: Scrambled Eggs with Turmeric and Veggies (p.26)
- Lunch: Mediterranean Hummus Plate (p.38)
- Dinner: Grilled Chicken with Quinoa and Roasted Broccoli (p.69)
- Snack: Greek Yogurt with Turmeric and Honey (p.103)

Saturday
- Breakfast: Quinoa Porridge with Almond Butter and Sliced Apples (p.28)
- Lunch: Mushroom and Spinach Whole Grain Wrap (p.41)
- Dinner: Stuffed Bell Peppers with Lentils and Brown Rice (p.71)
- Snack: Edamame with a Dash of Sea Salt (p.105)

Sunday

- Breakfast: Chia Pudding with Coconut Milk and Raspberries (p.29)
- Lunch: Warm Farro Salad with Broccoli, Peas, and Lemon-Tahini Dressing (p.42)
- Dinner: Miso Soup with Tofu and Seaweed (p.46)
- Snack: Banana Nice Cream (p.112)

Week 2

Monday
- Breakfast: Cottage Cheese with Pineapple and Ground Flaxseed (p.27)
- Lunch: Grilled Chicken and Sweet Potato Bowl (p.39)
- Dinner: Moroccan-Spiced Chicken Thighs with Roasted Carrots (p.78)
- Snack: Hummus with Carrot and Cucumber Sticks (p.99)

Tuesday
- Breakfast: Smoothie with Spinach, Blueberries, Banana, and Flaxseeds (p.25)
- Lunch: Mediterranean Chickpea Stew (p.50)
- Dinner: Grilled Mackerel with Avocado Slaw (p.73)
- Snack: Handful of Pumpkin Seeds or Sunflower Seeds (p.101)

Wednesday
- Breakfast: Avocado Toast on Whole Grain Bread (p.24)
- Lunch: Brown Rice Sushi Rolls with Veggies and Avocado (p.40)
- Dinner: Eggplant and Mushroom Stir-Fry over Brown Rice (p.76)
- Snack: Coconut Yogurt Parfait with Almonds and Blueberries (p.113)

Thursday
- Breakfast: Green Tea with a Side of Whole Grain Toast and Hummus (p.30)
- Lunch: Avocado and Citrus Spinach Salad (p.55)
- Dinner: Chickpea and Kale Stir-Fry with Olive Oil and Garlic (p.37)
- Snack: Avocado on Whole Grain Crackers (p.102)

Friday
- Breakfast: Greek Yogurt with Chia Seeds and Strawberries (p.23)
- Lunch: Hearty Vegetable and Quinoa Stew (p.45)
- Dinner: Farro Bowl with Roasted Veggies and Lemon-Herb Dressing (p.79)
- Snack: Chia Pudding with Cinnamon and Berries (p.100)

Saturday
- Breakfast: Chia Pudding with Coconut Milk and Raspberries (p.29)
- Lunch: Cabbage and Apple Slaw with Almonds (p.57)
- Dinner: Baked Tofu with Sweet Potato and Broccoli (p.77)
- Snack: Dark Chocolate-Dipped Strawberries (p.108)

Sunday
- Breakfast: Quinoa Porridge with Almond Butter and Sliced Apples (p.28)
- Lunch: Wild Rice and Cranberry Salad (p.59)

- Dinner: Tomato and White Bean Stew with Rosemary (p.49)
- Snack: Poached Pears with Ginger and Lemon (p.115)

Week 3

Monday
- Breakfast: Smoothie with Spinach, Blueberries, Banana, and Flaxseeds (p.25)
- Lunch: Mushroom and Spinach Whole Grain Wrap (p.41)
- Dinner: Miso-Glazed Cod with Steamed Greens and Brown Rice (p.80)
- Snack: Date and Nut Energy Bites (p.117)

Tuesday
- Breakfast: Scrambled Eggs with Turmeric and Veggies (p.26)
- Lunch: Warm Sweet Potato and Spinach Salad (p.58)
- Dinner: Chicken and Kale Soup with Garlic and Olive Oil (p.47)
- Snack: Apple Slices with Almond Butter (p.98)

Wednesday
- Breakfast: Cottage Cheese with Pineapple and Ground Flaxseed (p.27)
- Lunch: Quinoa Bowl with Roasted Veggies and Tahini Dressing (p.35)
- Dinner: Ground Turkey and Sweet Potato Skillet (p.82)
- Snack: Almond Flour Brownies (p.114)

Thursday
- Breakfast: Chia Pudding with Coconut Milk and Raspberries (p.29)
- Lunch: Grilled Salmon Salad with Mixed Greens (p.56)
- Dinner: Curried Sweet Potato and Carrot Soup (p.48)
- Snack: Avocado Chocolate Mousse (p.111)

Friday
- Breakfast: Avocado Toast on Whole Grain Bread (p.24)
- Lunch: Broccoli and Cauliflower Crunch Salad (p.60)
- Dinner: Sweet Potato and Black Bean Tacos (p.70)
- Snack: Smoothie Pops (Banana, Berries, and Spinach) (p.106)

Saturday
- Breakfast: Green Tea with a Side of Whole Grain Toast and Hummus (p.30)
- Lunch: Warm Farro Salad with Broccoli, Peas, and Lemon-Tahini Dressing (p.42)
- Dinner: Turmeric Chicken and Vegetable Skillet (p.75)
- Snack: Cinnamon-Spiced Almond Milk (p.127)

Sunday
- Breakfast: Greek Yogurt with Chia Seeds and Strawberries (p.23)

- Lunch: Tomato and White Bean Stew with Rosemary (p.49)
- Dinner: Quinoa and Vegetable-Stuffed Portobello Mushrooms (p.81)
- Snack: Baked Apples with Walnuts and Maple Syrup (p.110)

Week 4

Monday
- Breakfast: Oatmeal with Berries and Walnuts (p.22)
- Lunch: Lentil and Vegetable Soup with Turmeric (p.34)
- Dinner: Wild-Caught Shrimp Stir-Fry with Bok Choy and Ginger (p.74)
- Snack: Fresh Berries with Walnuts (p.97)

Tuesday
- Breakfast: Quinoa Porridge with Almond Butter and Sliced Apples (p.28)
- Lunch: Mediterranean Hummus Plate (p.38)
- Dinner: Butternut Squash and Apple Soup with Ginger (p.51)
- Snack: Greek Yogurt with Turmeric and Honey (p.103)

Wednesday
- Breakfast: Smoothie with Spinach, Blueberries, Banana, and Flaxseeds (p.25)
- Lunch: Sardine and Avocado Wrap (p.36)
- Dinner: Roasted Cauliflower Steaks with Herb Sauce (p.83)
- Snack: Edamame with Sea Salt (p.105)

Thursday
- Breakfast: Chia Pudding with Coconut Milk and Raspberries (p.29)
- Lunch: Cabbage and Apple Slaw with Almonds (p.57)
- Dinner: Turmeric Ginger Lentil Soup (p.44)
- Snack: Coconut Yogurt Parfait with Almonds and Blueberries (p.113)

Friday
- Breakfast: Greek Yogurt with Chia Seeds and Strawberries (p.23)
- Lunch: Avocado and Citrus Spinach Salad (p.55)
- Dinner: Mediterranean Baked Cod with Tomatoes and Olives (p.84)
- Snack: Dark Chocolate-Dipped Strawberries (p.108)

Saturday
- Breakfast: Green Tea with Whole Grain Toast and Hummus (p.30)
- Lunch: Wild Rice and Cranberry Salad (p.59)
- Dinner: Stuffed Bell Peppers with Lentils and Brown Rice (p.71)
- Snack: Chia Seed Pudding with Berries and Cinnamon (p.109)

Sunday

ANDREA D. RATLIFF

- Breakfast: Smoothie with Spinach, Blueberries, Banana, and Flaxseeds (p.25)
- Lunch: Mushroom and Spinach Whole Grain Wrap (p.41)
- Dinner: Spiced Red Lentil and Spinach Stew (p.53)
- Snack: Poached Pears with Ginger and Lemon (p.115)

BREAKFAST

Oatmeal with Berries and Walnuts

Prep Time: 5 minutes

Cook Time: 5–10 minutes

Servings: 2

Ingredients:

1 cup rolled oats (gluten-free if needed)

2 cups unsweetened almond milk or water

1/2 teaspoon ground cinnamon

1 cup mixed berries (fresh or frozen: blueberries, strawberries, raspberries)

1/4 cup chopped walnuts

1–2 teaspoons pure maple syrup or honey (optional)

1/2 teaspoon vanilla extract (optional)

1. In a medium saucepan, bring almond milk or water to a boil.

2. Stir in the oats and reduce heat to a simmer.

3. Add cinnamon and cook for 5–7 minutes, stirring occasionally, until oats are tender and creamy.

4. Stir in vanilla extract (if using).

5. Remove from heat and divide into two bowls.

6. Top each bowl with mixed berries, chopped walnuts, and a drizzle of maple syrup or honey if desired.

Greek Yogurt with Chia Seeds and Strawberries

Prep Time: 5 minutes

(no cooking required)

Servings: 2

Ingredients:

1 cup plain, unsweetened Greek yogurt (look for live active cultures)

2 tablespoons chia seeds

1 cup fresh strawberries, sliced

1–2 teaspoons raw honey or pure maple syrup (optional)

1/2 teaspoon ground cinnamon (optional)

1 tablespoon chopped walnuts or slivered almonds (optional)

1. In a bowl, combine Greek yogurt and chia seeds. Stir well.

2. Let sit for 5 minutes to allow the chia seeds to swell slightly or refrigerate overnight for a pudding-like texture).

3. Top with sliced strawberries.

4. Drizzle with honey or maple syrup if desired.

5. Sprinkle with cinnamon and nuts if using.

6. Serve, or refrigerate for up to 24 hours.

Avocado Toast on Whole Grain Bread

Prep Time: 5 minutes

Cook Time: 2–3 minutes (to toast the bread)

Servings: 2

Ingredients:

2 slices whole grain or sprouted grain bread

1 ripe avocado

1/4 teaspoon ground turmeric

A pinch of freshly ground black pepper

A squeeze of fresh lemon juice

Sea salt, to taste

Optional toppings:

Sliced cherry tomatoes

Hemp seeds or crushed walnuts

Arugula or microgreens

1. Toast the slices of whole grain bread to your desired crispness.

2. While the bread is toasting, cut the avocado in half, remove the pit, and scoop the flesh into a bowl.

3. Mash the avocado with a fork until creamy. Stir in turmeric, black pepper, lemon juice, and a pinch of sea salt.

4. Spread the mashed avocado mixture evenly onto the toasted bread.

5. Top with optional extras like cherry tomatoes, hemp seeds, or microgreens.

6. Serve.

Smoothie with Spinach, Blueberries, Banana, and Flaxseeds

Prep Time: 5 minutes

Servings: 2

Ingredients:

1 cup fresh spinach or frozen

1 cup unsweetened almond milk

1 banana (preferably ripe)

1/2 cup frozen or fresh blueberries

1 tablespoon ground flaxseeds

1/2 teaspoon cinnamon

1–2 teaspoons pure maple syrup or honey

2–3 ice cubes

1. Add all ingredients to a blender.

2. Blend on high until smooth and creamy, about 30–60 seconds.

3. Taste and adjust sweetness if needed.

4. Pour into two glasses and serve.

Optional Boost: Add a scoop of unsweetened plain Greek yogurt for probiotics, or a handful of frozen cauliflower for extra fiber and creaminess.

Scrambled Eggs with Turmeric and Veggies

Prep Time: 5–10 minutes

Cook Time: 5–7 minutes

Servings: 2

Ingredients:

4 large eggs (preferably pasture-raised or organic)

1/4 teaspoon ground turmeric

A pinch of black pepper

1 tablespoon extra-virgin olive oil or avocado oil

1/2 cup chopped bell pepper (any color)

1/2 cup cherry tomatoes, halved

1 cup baby spinach

Sea salt, to taste

Optional: chopped fresh herbs like parsley or cilantro for garnish

1. Crack the eggs into a bowl. Add turmeric, black pepper, and a pinch of salt. Whisk until well combined.

2. Heat olive oil in a nonstick skillet over medium heat.

3. Add chopped bell peppers and sauté for 2–3 minutes.

4. Add cherry tomatoes and cook for another 1–2 minutes, until they soften slightly.

5. Stir in the spinach and let it wilt (about 30 seconds).

6. Pour in the egg mixture. Let it sit for a few seconds, then gently stir and fold the eggs until just cooked (about 2–3 minutes).

7. Remove from heat immediately to avoid overcooking. Garnish with fresh herbs if desired.

8. Serve warm, ideally with a slice of whole grain toast or a side of avocado.

Optional Boost: Add a sprinkle of hemp seeds or a few slices of avocado for healthy fats and extra anti-inflammatory nutrients.

Cottage Cheese with Pineapple and Ground Flaxseed

Prep Time: 5 minutes

Servings: 2

Ingredients:

1 cup low-fat or full-fat cottage cheese (look for live active cultures on the label)

1 cup fresh pineapple chunks or no-sugar-added canned pineapple in juice, drained

2 tablespoons ground flaxseed

1/2 teaspoon ground cinnamon (optional)

1–2 teaspoons raw honey or pure maple syrup

A few mint leaves for garnish (optional)

1. In a bowl, divide cottage cheese between two serving dishes.

2. Top each with pineapple chunks.

3. Sprinkle 1 tablespoon of ground flaxseed over each portion.

4. Add cinnamon and a drizzle of honey or maple syrup if desired.

5. Garnish with mint leaves and serve.

Optional Boost: Mix in a tablespoon of chopped walnuts or chia seeds.

Quinoa Porridge with Almond Butter and Sliced Apples

Prep Time: 5 minutes

Cook Time: 15–20 minutes

Servings: 2

Ingredients:

1/2 cup uncooked quinoa (rinsed well)

1 cup unsweetened almond milk or water

1/2 teaspoon ground cinnamon

1 medium apple, thinly sliced

2 tablespoons almond butter

1–2 teaspoons pure maple syrup or raw honey (optional)

1 tablespoon ground flaxseed or chia seeds

Pinch of sea salt

1. In a saucepan, combine rinsed quinoa, almond milk, cinnamon, and a pinch of salt. Bring to a boil.

2. Reduce heat to low, cover, and simmer for 15–18 minutes, or until quinoa is tender and most of the liquid is absorbed.

3. Stir in almond butter and maple syrup (if using) until well blended.

4. Divide porridge into two bowls. Top with sliced apples.

5. Sprinkle with ground flaxseed or chia seeds for extra omega-3s and fiber.

6. Serve warm.

Optional Boost: Add a splash of vanilla extract or a sprinkle of walnuts

Chia Pudding with Coconut Milk and Raspberries

Prep Time: 5 minutes

Chill Time: At least 4 hours or overnight

Servings: 2

Ingredients:

1/2 cup chia seeds

2 cups unsweetened coconut milk (from a carton or can)

1/2 teaspoon pure vanilla extract (optional)

1–2 teaspoons pure maple syrup or raw honey (optional)

1 cup fresh or frozen raspberries

1 tablespoon unsweetened shredded coconut

1. In a mixing bowl or jar, combine chia seeds, coconut milk, vanilla extract, and sweetener (if using). Stir well.

2. Let the mixture sit for 5 minutes, then stir again to prevent clumping.

3. Cover and refrigerate for at least 4 hours or overnight until it thickens to a pudding-like consistency.

4. When ready to serve, stir the pudding and divide into two bowls or jars.

5. Top with raspberries and a sprinkle of shredded coconut.

6. Enjoy chilled.

Optional Boost: Add a few chopped walnuts or a pinch of cinnamon

Green Tea with a Side of Whole Grain Toast and Hummus

Prep Time: 5 minutes

Cook Time: 2–3 minutes

Servings: 1

Ingredients:

1 green tea bag or 1 teaspoon loose-leaf green tea

1 cup hot water (not boiling — about 175°F or 80°C)

1 slice whole grain or sprouted grain bread

2–3 tablespoons hummus (store-bought or homemade)

Optional toppings: sliced cucumber, cherry tomatoes, arugula, or a sprinkle of paprika

1. Heat water to just below boiling and steep green tea for 2–3 minutes. Remove tea bag or strain leaves.

2. Toast the bread to desired crispness.

3. Spread hummus generously on the toast.

4. Top with optional sliced veggies or greens for added nutrients and color.

5. Serve toast with your cup of green tea on the side.

Optional Boost: Add a drizzle of extra virgin olive oil and a pinch of ground cumin or turmeric to the hummus.

Sweet Potato Hash with Kale and Olive Oil

Prep Time: 10 minutes

Cook Time: 15–20 minutes

Servings: 2

Ingredients:

1 large sweet potato, peeled and diced into ½-inch cubes

1 tablespoon extra-virgin olive oil

1/2 small red onion, thinly sliced

2 cups chopped kale (ribs removed)

1 clove garlic, minced

1/4 teaspoon smoked paprika (optional)

Sea salt and freshly ground black pepper, to taste

Optional: squeeze of fresh lemon juice

1. In a large skillet, heat olive oil over medium heat.

2. Add diced sweet potato and sauté for about 8–10 minutes, stirring occasionally, until starting to soften and brown.

3. Add red onion and cook for another 3–4 minutes until translucent.

4. Stir in garlic and smoked paprika (if using), then add chopped kale.

5. Continue cooking for 3–5 minutes, until kale is wilted and sweet potatoes are tender.

6. Season with salt, pepper, and a splash of lemon juice if desired.

7. Serve hot, either on its own or topped with a fried or poached egg for added protein.

Optional Boost: Sprinkle with hemp seeds or pumpkin seeds.

ANDREA D. RATLIFF

Lunch

Grilled Salmon Salad with Olive Oil Vinaigrette

Prep Time: 10 minutes

Cook Time: 10–12 minutes

Servings: 2

Ingredients:

For the Salad:

2 wild-caught salmon fillets (about 4–5 oz each)

4 cups mixed leafy greens (spinach, arugula, kale, or romaine)

1/2 avocado, sliced

1/2 cucumber, thinly sliced

1/2 red bell pepper, sliced

2 tablespoons chopped walnuts

Sea salt and black pepper, to taste

Optional: lemon wedges for serving

For the Vinaigrette:

2 tablespoons extra virgin olive oil

1 tablespoon fresh lemon juice or apple cider vinegar

1/2 teaspoon Dijon mustard

1/2 teaspoon honey or maple syrup (optional)

Pinch of sea salt and black pepper

1. Season salmon with sea salt and pepper. Grill on medium-high heat (skin side down if applicable) for 4–5 minutes per side, or until it flakes easily with a fork.

2. In a small jar or bowl, whisk together olive oil, lemon juice, mustard, honey, salt, and pepper until well combined.

3. Divide greens between two plates. Top with avocado, cucumber, red bell pepper, and walnuts.

4. Place grilled salmon on top of each salad. Drizzle with vinaigrette and serve with lemon wedges if desired.

Optional Boost: Sprinkle with hemp seeds or microgreens.

Lentil and Vegetable Soup with Turmeric

Prep Time: 10 minutes

Cook Time: 30–35 minutes

Servings: 4

Ingredients:

1 tablespoon extra-virgin olive oil

1 small onion, chopped

2 cloves garlic, minced

2 carrots, diced

2 celery stalks, diced

1 teaspoon ground turmeric

1/4 teaspoon ground black pepper

1 cup dry brown or green lentils (rinsed)

1 can (14.5 oz) diced tomatoes (no salt added, if possible)

5 cups low-sodium vegetable broth or water

2 cups fresh spinach or kale

1 teaspoon sea salt

Juice of 1/2 lemon

Fresh herbs like parsley or cilantro for garnish (optional)

1. Heat olive oil in a large pot over medium heat. Add onion and garlic; sauté for 2–3 minutes until softened.

2. Add carrots and celery, and cook for another 5 minutes.

3. Stir in turmeric and black pepper, letting them bloom in the oil for about 1 minute.

4. Add lentils, diced tomatoes (with their juices), and broth. Bring to a boil.

5. Reduce heat to low, cover, and simmer for 25–30 minutes, or until lentils are tender.

6. Stir in spinach and cook for another 2–3 minutes until wilted.

7. Adjust seasoning with salt and lemon juice. Serve hot, garnished with herbs if desired.

Optional Boost: Add 1 teaspoon of grated fresh ginger.

Quinoa Bowl with Roasted Veggies and Tahini Dressing

Prep Time: 10 minutes

Cook Time: 25–30 minutes

Servings: 2

Ingredients:

For the Bowl:

1/2 cup uncooked quinoa (rinsed)

1 cup water or low-sodium vegetable broth

1 small zucchini, sliced

1/2 eggplant, cubed

1 bell pepper, chopped

1 tablespoon extra-virgin olive oil

1/2 teaspoon ground cumin

1/2 teaspoon smoked paprika

Salt and pepper, to taste

For the Tahini Dressing:

2 tablespoons tahini

1 tablespoon lemon juice

1 tablespoon warm water (more as needed to thin)

1 small garlic clove, minced (optional)

Pinch of sea salt

Pinch of turmeric

1. Roast the veggies:

Preheat oven to 400°F (200°C).

Toss zucchini, eggplant, and bell pepper in olive oil, cumin, paprika, salt, and pepper.

Spread on a baking sheet and roast for 20–25 minutes, flipping halfway.

2. Cook the quinoa:

In a saucepan, combine rinsed quinoa and water or broth.

Bring to a boil, then reduce heat to low, cover, and simmer for 15 minutes.

Remove from heat and let sit covered for 5 minutes. Fluff with a fork.

3. Whisk tahini, lemon juice, water, garlic (if using), salt, and turmeric until smooth and creamy. Add more water to thin as needed.

4. Assemble the bowl:

Divide quinoa into two bowls.

Top with roasted veggies and drizzle generously with tahini dressing.

Serve warm or at room temperature.

Optional Boost: Garnish with chopped parsley, pumpkin seeds, or a few pomegranate arils.

Sardine and Avocado Wrap (in Whole Grain or Lettuce Wrap)

Prep Time: 10 minutes

Servings: 2

Ingredients:

1 can (3.75 oz) sardines in olive oil or water, drained

1 ripe avocado

2 whole grain wraps or 4 large romaine or collard leaves

1/2 small cucumber, thinly sliced

1/2 small red bell pepper, sliced thin

1 tablespoon fresh lemon juice

Sea salt and black pepper, to taste

Optional: a pinch of turmeric, handful of sprouts or arugula, or a drizzle of olive oil

1. In a bowl, mash the avocado with lemon juice, salt, pepper, and turmeric (if using).

2. Spread the mashed avocado on each wrap or leafy green.

3. Layer with sardines, cucumber, and bell pepper slices.

4. Add sprouts or arugula for extra crunch and nutrients.

5. Roll up the whole grain wrap or fold the lettuce around the filling.

6. Serve immediately or wrap tightly and refrigerate for up to 24 hours.

Optional Boost: Add a smear of hummus or a sprinkle of hemp seeds for added fiber and healthy fats.

Chickpea and Kale Stir-Fry with Olive Oil and Garlic

Prep Time: 10 minutes

Cook Time: 10 minutes

Servings: 2

Ingredients:

1 tablespoon extra-virgin olive oil

2 garlic cloves, minced

1 can (15 oz) chickpeas, drained and rinsed

4 cups chopped kale (stems removed)

1/4 teaspoon sea salt or to taste

1/4 teaspoon black pepper

Juice of 1/2 lemon

Pinch of red pepper flakes

1. Heat olive oil in a large skillet over medium heat.

2. Add minced garlic and sauté for about 30 seconds until fragrant, being careful not to burn it.

3. Add chickpeas and cook for 3–4 minutes, stirring occasionally, until lightly browned.

4. Add chopped kale, salt, and pepper. Stir well and cook for 4–5 minutes, until the kale is wilted and tender.

5. Finish with a squeeze of lemon juice and red pepper flakes if desired.

6. Serve warm, as a main dish or a hearty side.

Optional Boost: Add a spoonful of tahini or a sprinkle of hemp seeds on top.

Mediterranean Hummus Plate

Prep Time: 10 minutes

Servings: 2

Ingredients:

For the Plate:

1 cup hummus (store-bought or homemade; see below)

1 cup cherry tomatoes, halved

1 small cucumber, sliced into rounds or sticks

1/4 cup Kalamata or black olives

1–2 whole grain pitas, cut into wedges or use gluten-free crackers or seed crackers

Optional: sprinkle of paprika or za'atar, lemon wedges

For Homemade Hummus:

1 can (15 oz) chickpeas, drained and rinsed

2 tablespoons tahini

2 tablespoons extra virgin olive oil

Juice of 1 lemon

1 small garlic clove (optional)

1/4 teaspoon sea salt

2–4 tablespoons water (to thin)

1. If making hummus: Combine chickpeas, tahini, olive oil, lemon juice, garlic, and salt in a food processor. Blend until smooth, adding water gradually until creamy. Taste and adjust seasoning.

2. Arrange hummus in the center of a large plate or shallow bowl.

3. Surround with cucumber slices, cherry tomatoes, olives, and pita wedges or crackers.

4. Garnish with paprika, za'atar, or a drizzle of olive oil, if desired.

5. Serve or chill for up to 1 day.

Optional Boost: Add sliced avocado or artichoke hearts.

Grilled Chicken and Sweet Potato Bowl

Prep Time: 10–15 minutes

Cook Time: 25–30 minutes

Servings: 2

Ingredients:

2 boneless, skinless chicken breasts

1 medium sweet potato, peeled and cubed

2 cups fresh arugula

2 tablespoons pumpkin seeds (pepitas)

1 tablespoon extra-virgin olive oil (plus more for drizzling)

1/2 teaspoon smoked paprika

1/2 teaspoon garlic powder

Salt and black pepper to taste

Juice of 1/2 lemon or a splash of apple cider vinegar (optional)

1. Roast the Sweet Potatoes:

Preheat oven to 400°F (200°C).

Toss sweet potato cubes with 1/2 tablespoon olive oil, paprika, garlic powder, salt, and pepper.

Spread on a baking sheet and roast for 20–25 minutes, flipping halfway, until tender and golden.

2. Grill the Chicken:

While sweet potatoes roast, heat a grill pan or outdoor grill over medium heat.

Rub chicken breasts with 1/2 tablespoon olive oil, salt, and pepper.

Grill for 5–7 minutes per side, or until fully cooked (internal temp 165°F/74°C).

Let it rest, then slice.

3. Assemble the Bowls:

Divide arugula between two bowls.

Top each with sweet potatoes, sliced grilled chicken, and pumpkin seeds.

Drizzle with a touch of olive oil and lemon juice or vinegar before serving.

Optional Boost: Add a spoonful of hummus, sliced avocado, or fermented veggies (like kimchi).

Brown Rice Sushi Rolls with Veggies and Avocado

Prep Time: 20 minutes

Cook Time: 30–40 minutes (for rice)

Servings: 2–3 (makes about 4 rolls)

Ingredients:

1 cup short-grain brown rice, rinsed

2 cups water

1 tablespoon rice vinegar

4 nori sheets (seaweed)

1 ripe avocado, sliced

1 small cucumber, julienned

1 small carrot, peeled and julienned

1/2 red bell pepper, thinly sliced

A handful of baby spinach or arugula

Optional: pickled ginger, sesame seeds, or a dash of low-sodium tamari

1. In a saucepan, combine brown rice and water. Bring to a boil, then reduce to a simmer, cover, and cook for 30–35 minutes until tender. Let rest for 10 minutes. Stir in rice vinegar if using, and cool slightly.

2. While rice is cooking, slice veggies and avocado.

3. Assemble the rolls:

Place a nori sheet shiny side down on a bamboo mat or clean surface.

Spread a thin layer of rice (about 3/4 cup) over the bottom 2/3 of the sheet, leaving the top edge bare.

Layer your veggies and avocado horizontally across the center.

Roll tightly from the bottom using light pressure. Wet the top edge with a little water to seal the roll.

4. Use a sharp, damp knife to slice into 6–8 pieces per roll. Serve with pickled ginger or a side of tamari if desired.

Optional Boost: Sprinkle sesame seeds on top or mix turmeric into the rice.

Mushroom and Spinach Whole Grain Wrap

Prep Time: 10 minutes

Cook Time: 7–10 minutes

Servings: 2 wraps

Ingredients:

1 tablespoon extra-virgin olive oil or avocado oil

1 cup cremini or shiitake mushrooms, sliced

2 cups fresh baby spinach

1 garlic clove, minced

1/2 teaspoon dried oregano or thyme

Pinch of sea salt and black pepper, to taste

2 whole grain or sprouted grain tortillas

Optional spread: 2 tablespoons hummus or mashed avocado

Optional toppings: sliced red onion, shredded carrots, or sprouts

1. Heat oil in a skillet over medium heat.

2. Add mushrooms and cook for 5–6 minutes until softened and lightly browned.

3. Add garlic (if using) and spinach. Cook another 1–2 minutes until spinach wilts.

4. Season with oregano, salt, and pepper.

5. Warm tortillas slightly, then spread with hummus or avocado if using.

6. Divide mushroom-spinach mixture between the wraps.

7. Add optional toppings, then roll up tightly. Serve warm or at room temperature.

Optional Boost: Add a pinch of turmeric and black pepper during cooking.

ANDREA D. RATLIFF

Warm Farro Salad with Broccoli, Peas, and Lemon-Tahini Dressing

Prep Time: 10 minutes

Cook Time: 20 minutes

Servings: 2–3

Ingredients:

For the salad:

1/2 cup uncooked farro (rinsed)

1 1/2 cups water or low-sodium vegetable broth

1 cup broccoli florets

1/2 cup green peas (fresh or frozen)

1 tablespoon extra-virgin olive oil

Sea salt, to taste

For the lemon-tahini dressing:

2 tablespoons tahini

Juice of 1 lemon (about 2 tablespoons)

1 tablespoon warm water

1 small garlic clove, grated or minced

1/2 teaspoon ground cumin

Pinch of sea salt

1. In a medium pot, combine farro and water/broth. Bring to a boil, then reduce heat to simmer. Cover and cook for 20 minutes or until tender. Drain any excess water.

2. While farro cooks, steam or lightly sauté broccoli florets and peas until just tender (about 5 minutes).

3. In a small bowl, whisk together tahini, lemon juice, warm water, garlic, cumin (if using), and salt until smooth. Add more water if needed to thin the dressing.

4. In a large bowl, combine cooked farro, broccoli, and peas. Drizzle with olive oil and toss to coat.

5. Pour the lemon-tahini dressing over the salad and mix well.

6. Serve warm or at room temperature.

Optional Boost: Top with toasted sunflower seeds, pumpkin seeds, or chopped parsley.

Soups and Stews

ANDREA D. RATLIFF

Turmeric Ginger Lentil Soup

Prep Time: 10 minutes

Cook Time: 30–35 minutes

Servings: 4

Ingredients:

1 tablespoon extra-virgin olive oil

1 small onion, chopped

2 cloves garlic, minced

1 tablespoon fresh ginger, grated or 1 tsp ground ginger

1 teaspoon ground turmeric

1/2 teaspoon ground cumin

2 carrots, diced

2 celery stalks, diced

3/4 cup dried red or green lentils, rinsed

4 cups low-sodium vegetable broth

2 cups baby spinach

Sea salt and black pepper, to taste

Juice of 1/2 lemon

Fresh cilantro or parsley for garnish (optional)

1. In a large pot, heat olive oil over medium heat. Add chopped onion and sauté until translucent (about 3–4 minutes).

2. Stir in garlic, ginger, turmeric, and cumin. Cook for 1 minute until fragrant.

3. Add carrots, celery, and lentils. Stir to coat in the spices.

4. Pour in vegetable broth and bring to a boil. Reduce heat and simmer for 25–30 minutes, or until lentils are soft.

5. Stir in spinach and cook for another 2–3 minutes until wilted.

6. Season with salt, pepper, and lemon juice if using.

7. Serve hot, garnished with fresh herbs if desired.

Optional Boost: Add a small pinch of cayenne pepper..

Hearty Vegetable and Quinoa Stew

Prep Time: 10–15 minutes

Cook Time: 25–30 minutes

Servings: 4

Ingredients:

For the salad:

1/2 cup uncooked farro (rinsed)

1 1/2 cups water or low-sodium vegetable broth

1 cup broccoli florets

1/2 cup green peas (fresh or frozen)

1 tablespoon extra-virgin olive oil

Sea salt, to taste

For the lemon-tahini dressing:

2 tablespoons tahini

Juice of 1 lemon (about 2 tablespoons)

1 tablespoon warm water

1 small garlic clove, grated or minced

1/2 teaspoon ground cumin

Pinch of sea salt

1. Heat olive oil in a large pot over medium heat. Add onion and garlic, sauté for 2–3 minutes.

2. Stir in bell pepper, zucchini, carrot, and turmeric. Cook for another 5 minutes, stirring occasionally.

3. Add tomatoes, quinoa, broth, cumin, black pepper, and a pinch of salt.

4. Bring to a boil, then reduce heat and simmer covered for 20 minutes, or until quinoa is cooked and vegetables are tender.

5. Stir in spinach or kale (if using) and let wilt for 2–3 minutes.

6. Add lemon juice, adjust seasoning to taste, and serve hot.

Optional Boost: Top with chopped parsley, avocado slices, or a sprinkle of hemp seeds.

Miso Soup with Tofu and Seaweed

Prep Time: 5 minutes

Cook Time: 10 minutes

Servings: 2

Ingredients:

3 cups water

2 tablespoons white or yellow miso paste (look for unpasteurized, refrigerated miso for live cultures)

1/2 cup cubed silken or soft tofu

1 tablespoon dried wakame seaweed or substitute with other edible seaweed, rehydrated

1 green onion, thinly sliced

Optional: 1 teaspoon grated fresh ginger or a small piece of kombu (sea kelp)

1. In a medium saucepan, bring water to a gentle simmer (not a full boil, which can damage probiotics).

2. If using kombu or ginger, add it now and let simmer for 3–5 minutes. Then remove kombu if used.

3. Stir in miso paste, whisking gently to dissolve completely.

4. Add tofu cubes and wakame seaweed. Simmer for another 2–3 minutes, until the seaweed expands and tofu is heated through.

5. Remove from heat. Stir in green onions just before serving.

6. Pour into bowls and enjoy warm.

Optional Boost: Add a handful of spinach or a few shiitake mushrooms..

Chicken and Kale Soup with Garlic and Olive Oil

Prep Time: 10–15 minutes

Cook Time: 30–35 minutes

Servings: 4

Ingredients:

1 tablespoon extra virgin olive oil

4 cloves garlic, minced

1 small yellow onion, diced

2 carrots, sliced

2 celery stalks, sliced

6 cups low-sodium chicken broth (preferably homemade or bone broth)

2 cups cooked shredded chicken (breast or thigh, skinless)

3 cups chopped kale (stems removed)

1/2 teaspoon dried thyme

Sea salt and black pepper, to taste

Optional: juice of 1/2 lemon

1. Heat olive oil in a large pot over medium heat. Add garlic and onion, sauté for 2–3 minutes until fragrant.

2. Add carrots and celery. Cook for another 5 minutes, stirring occasionally.

3. Pour in chicken broth and bring to a boil. Reduce heat to low and simmer for 10 minutes.

4. Add shredded chicken, kale, thyme, salt, and pepper. Simmer another 10–15 minutes, until kale is tender and flavors are blended.

5. Finish with lemon juice, if using. Adjust seasoning as needed.

6. Serve hot, optionally with a slice of whole grain toast or a spoonful of cooked quinoa.

Optional Boost: Add a pinch of turmeric and a crack of black pepper with the garlic..

Curried Sweet Potato and Carrot Soup

Prep Time: 10 minutes

Cook Time: 25–30 minutes

Servings: 4

Ingredients:

1 tablespoon extra-virgin olive oil

1 medium onion, chopped

2 cloves garlic, minced

1 tablespoon fresh ginger, grated or 1 teaspoon ground ginger

2 teaspoons ground turmeric

1 teaspoon ground cumin

2 medium carrots, peeled and chopped

1 large sweet potato, peeled and cubed

4 cups low-sodium vegetable broth or bone broth

1/2 cup full-fat coconut milk

Sea salt and black pepper, to taste

Fresh cilantro or parsley for garnish

1. Heat olive oil in a large pot over medium heat. Add onion and sauté for 3–4 minutes, until translucent.

2. Stir in garlic, ginger, turmeric, and cumin. Cook for 1 minute until fragrant.

3. Add chopped carrots and sweet potato. Stir to coat in the spices.

4. Pour in broth and bring to a boil. Reduce heat, cover, and simmer for 20–25 minutes, until vegetables are soft.

5. Use an immersion blender to puree the soup in the pot (or carefully transfer to a blender in batches).

6. Stir in coconut milk if using, and season with salt and pepper to taste.

7. Serve hot, garnished with fresh herbs if desired.

Optional Boost: Add a pinch of cayenne for gentle heat.

Tomato and White Bean Stew with Rosemary

Prep Time: 10 minutes

Cook Time: 25–30 minutes

Servings: 4

Ingredients:

1 tablespoon extra-virgin olive oil

1 small yellow onion, finely chopped

2 garlic cloves, minced

1 medium carrot, diced

1 celery stalk, diced

1 can (15 oz) diced tomatoes (no salt added)

1 can (15 oz) white beans (like cannellini or navy), drained and rinsed

1 cup low-sodium vegetable broth or water

1 teaspoon fresh rosemary, finely chopped or 1/2 teaspoon dried

1/2 teaspoon dried thyme (optional)

Salt and freshly ground black pepper, to taste

1 handful of fresh spinach or kale

Fresh lemon juice, for serving

1. In a large saucepan, heat olive oil over medium heat.
2. Add onion, carrot, and celery. Sauté for 5–7 minutes until soft.
3. Stir in garlic and rosemary. Cook for 1 minute until fragrant.
4. Add diced tomatoes, white beans, and vegetable broth. Stir to combine.
5. Bring to a gentle simmer, cover, and cook for 15–20 minutes.
6. Stir in greens (if using) and cook for another 2–3 minutes until wilted.
7. Season with salt, pepper, and a splash of lemon juice to brighten flavors.
8. Serve warm, optionally with a slice of whole grain bread.

Optional Boost: Add a pinch of crushed red pepper flakes..

ANDREA D. RATLIFF

Mediterranean Chickpea Stew

Prep Time: 10 minutes

Cook Time: 25 minutes

Servings: 4

Ingredients:

2 tablespoons extra virgin olive oil

1 small onion, diced

2 cloves garlic, minced

1 teaspoon ground cumin

1/2 teaspoon smoked paprika

1/4 teaspoon ground turmeric

1 (15 oz) can no-salt-added chickpeas, drained and rinsed

1 (15 oz) can diced tomatoes (BPA-free lining preferred)

2 cups low-sodium vegetable broth

2 cups baby spinach

Salt and black pepper, to taste

Juice of 1/2 lemon

Fresh parsley for garnish

1. In a medium pot, heat olive oil over medium heat. Add onion and sauté for 3–4 minutes until soft.

2. Add garlic, cumin, paprika, and turmeric. Stir for 30 seconds until fragrant.

3. Add chickpeas, diced tomatoes (with juice), and broth. Bring to a gentle boil.

4. Reduce heat and simmer uncovered for 15–20 minutes, until slightly thickened.

5. Stir in spinach and cook another 1–2 minutes until wilted.

6. Season with salt, pepper, and lemon juice to taste.

7. Serve warm, topped with fresh parsley if desired.

Optional Boost: Add chopped zucchini, bell pepper, or carrots..

Butternut Squash and Apple Soup with Ginger

Prep Time: 10–15 minutes

Cook Time: 25–30 minutes

Servings: 4

Ingredients:

1 tablespoon extra-virgin olive oil

1 small onion, chopped

2 teaspoons fresh ginger, grated or 1/2 tsp ground ginger

3 cups butternut squash, peeled and cubed

1 medium apple (e.g., Honeycrisp or Fuji), peeled, cored, and chopped

3 cups low-sodium vegetable broth

1/2 teaspoon ground cinnamon

Sea salt and black pepper, to taste

1/4 cup canned light coconut milk or almond milk

Fresh thyme or pumpkin seeds for garnish

1. Heat olive oil in a large pot over medium heat. Add chopped onion and sauté until soft, about 5 minutes.

2. Stir in grated ginger and cook for 1 minute.

3. Add butternut squash and apple. Stir to coat with the aromatics.

4. Pour in vegetable broth and bring to a boil. Reduce heat and simmer uncovered for 20–25 minutes, until squash is very tender.

5. Remove from heat. Use an immersion blender to purée the soup until smooth, or transfer carefully to a blender in batches.

6. Stir in coconut or almond milk if using, and season with salt and pepper to taste.

7. Serve warm, garnished with fresh thyme or pumpkin seeds if desired.

Optional Boost: Add a pinch of turmeric..

ANDREA D. RATLIFF

Wild Rice and Mushroom Soup

Prep Time: 10 minutes

Cook Time: 40–45 minutes

Servings: 4

Ingredients:

1 tablespoon extra-virgin olive oil

1 small yellow onion, diced

2 garlic cloves, minced

2 cups mixed mushrooms, sliced (e.g., cremini, shiitake, or button)

3/4 cup wild rice, rinsed

1 medium carrot, diced

1 celery stalk, diced

4 cups low-sodium vegetable broth

1/2 teaspoon dried thyme

1/2 teaspoon ground turmeric

Sea salt and freshly ground black pepper, to taste

1 cup unsweetened almond milk or oat milk

1 tablespoon chopped fresh parsley (for garnish)

1. In a large pot, heat olive oil over medium heat. Add onion and garlic; sauté for 2–3 minutes until fragrant.

2. Add mushrooms, carrots, and celery. Cook for 5–7 minutes, until softened.

3. Stir in wild rice, thyme, turmeric (if using), and vegetable broth.

4. Bring to a boil, then reduce heat, cover, and simmer for 35–40 minutes, or until rice is tender.

5. If a creamier soup is desired, stir in almond or oat milk and heat through.

6. Season with salt and pepper to taste.

7. Serve hot, garnished with fresh parsley.

Optional Boost: Add a handful of chopped kale or spinach during the last 5 minutes of cooking..

.

Spiced Red Lentil and Spinach Stew

Prep Time: 10 minutes

Cook Time: 25–30 minutes

Servings: 4

Ingredients:

1 tablespoon extra-virgin olive oil

1 small onion, finely chopped

2 cloves garlic, minced

1 teaspoon ground turmeric

1 teaspoon smoked paprika or regular paprika

1/2 teaspoon ground cumin

1 cup red lentils (rinsed well)

1 medium carrot, diced

1/2 teaspoon sea salt (adjust to taste)

1/4 teaspoon black pepper

4 cups low-sodium vegetable broth or water

2 cups fresh baby spinach or 1 cup frozen spinach

Juice of half a lemon

Fresh cilantro or parsley for garnish

1. Heat olive oil in a large pot over medium heat. Add onion and sauté for 3–4 minutes, until soft and translucent.

2. Add garlic, turmeric, paprika, and cumin. Stir for 1 minute until fragrant.

3. Add red lentils, carrot, salt, and black pepper. Stir to coat.

4. Pour in the vegetable broth. Bring to a boil, then reduce heat and simmer uncovered for 20–25 minutes, until lentils are tender and stew thickens.

5. Stir in spinach and simmer for another 2–3 minutes until wilted.

6. Finish with a squeeze of lemon juice if desired.

7. Serve hot, garnished with fresh herbs.

Optional Boost: Add a pinch of cayenne pepper or a spoonful of plain yogurt (if tolerated)..

ANDREA D. RATLIFF

Salads and Dressings

Avocado and Citrus Spinach Salad

Prep Time: 10 minutes

Servings: 2

Ingredients:

4 cups baby spinach

1 large orange, peeled and sliced into rounds or segments

1 ripe avocado, sliced

1/4 small red onion, thinly sliced

2 tablespoons sunflower seeds (raw or lightly toasted)

For the dressing (optional but recommended):

2 tablespoons extra virgin olive oil

1 tablespoon fresh lemon juice or orange juice

1/2 teaspoon Dijon mustard

Sea salt and black pepper, to taste

1. In a large bowl or serving platter, layer the baby spinach, orange slices, avocado, and red onion.

2. Sprinkle with sunflower seeds.

3. In a small bowl, whisk together the olive oil, lemon/orange juice, mustard, salt, and pepper.

4. Drizzle dressing over salad just before serving.

5. Gently toss or leave arranged as-is for a pretty presentation.

Optional Boost: Add hemp hearts or a few pomegranate seeds.

ANDREA D. RATLIFF

Grilled Salmon Salad with Mixed Greens

Prep Time: 10 minutes

Cook Time: 10–12 minutes (grilling the salmon)

Servings: 2

Ingredients:

2 salmon fillets (about 4–5 oz each, skin-on or skinless)

4 cups mixed greens (spinach, arugula, kale, romaine, etc.)

1/2 cup cherry tomatoes, halved

1/2 cucumber, thinly sliced

1/4 cup pitted Kalamata olives or green olives

2 tablespoons extra virgin olive oil

1 tablespoon lemon juice

1/2 teaspoon dried oregano or dill (optional)

Sea salt and black pepper, to taste

1. Grill the salmon:

Preheat a grill or grill pan over medium-high heat.

Season salmon with salt, pepper, and a drizzle of olive oil.

Grill for 4–5 minutes per side, or until cooked through and flaky. Set aside to cool slightly.

2. In a large bowl, combine mixed greens, cherry tomatoes, cucumber, and olives.

3. Dress the salad:

In a small bowl, whisk together olive oil, lemon juice, and oregano (if using).

Drizzle over the salad and toss gently.

4. Place the grilled salmon on top of the salad. Serve warm or room temperature.

Optional Boost: Top with a sprinkle of hemp seeds or a few slices of avocado.

Cabbage and Apple Slaw with Almonds

Prep Time: 10 minutes

Servings: 4

Ingredients:

2 cups shredded red cabbage

1 green apple, julienned or thinly sliced

1/4 cup sliced almonds (lightly toasted for extra flavor, optional)

2 tablespoons fresh lemon juice

1 tablespoon extra-virgin olive oil

Pinch of sea salt

Freshly ground black pepper, to taste

1. In a large mixing bowl, combine shredded cabbage and sliced apple.

2. Add lemon juice, olive oil (if using), salt, and pepper. Toss until evenly coated.

3. Top with sliced almonds just before serving for crunch.

4. Serve or refrigerate for up to 24 hours (flavors will mellow).

Optional Boost: Add chopped parsley or a dash of apple cider vinegar.

Warm Sweet Potato and Spinach Salad

Prep Time: 10 minutes

Cook Time: 25–30 minutes

Servings: 2

Ingredients:

2 medium sweet potatoes, peeled and cut into 1-inch cubes

1 tablespoon extra-virgin olive oil

1/4 teaspoon ground cumin

Sea salt and black pepper, to taste

3 cups baby spinach

2 scallions, thinly sliced

2 tablespoons pumpkin seeds (raw or lightly toasted)

Juice of 1/2 lemon or 1 tablespoon apple cider vinegar

1. Preheat oven to 400°F (200°C). Toss sweet potato cubes with olive oil, cumin (if using), salt, and pepper. Spread on a baking sheet and roast for 25–30 minutes, flipping halfway through, until golden and tender.

2. Place spinach in a large bowl. Once sweet potatoes are done, add them to the spinach while still warm to slightly wilt the greens.

3. Sprinkle in scallions and pumpkin seeds. Drizzle with lemon juice or apple cider vinegar. Toss gently and serve warm or at room temperature.

Optional Boost: Add a spoonful of hummus or tahini on top.

Wild Rice and Cranberry Salad

Prep Time: 10 minutes

Cook Time: 45 minutes (for wild rice)

Servings: 4

Ingredients:

1 cup uncooked wild rice

2 cups water or low-sodium vegetable broth

1/2 cup unsweetened dried cranberries

1/2 cup chopped celery

1/4 cup chopped green onions

1/3 cup chopped pecans (toasted, optional)

2 tablespoons extra virgin olive oil

1 tablespoon apple cider vinegar or lemon juice

Sea salt and black pepper, to taste

Optional: 1 teaspoon Dijon mustard or 1/2 teaspoon maple syrup for dressing depth

1. Rinse wild rice under cold water. In a saucepan, combine with water or broth and bring to a boil.

2. Reduce heat, cover, and simmer for 40–45 minutes, or until rice is tender and some grains have split open. Drain excess liquid if needed and let cool slightly.

3. In a large bowl, combine cooked wild rice, cranberries, celery, green onions, and pecans.

4. In a small bowl, whisk together olive oil, vinegar (or lemon juice), salt, pepper, and optional Dijon/maple syrup.

5. Pour dressing over the salad and toss gently to combine.

6. Serve warm, at room temperature, or chilled.

Optional Boost: Add a handful of chopped parsley or arugula.

Broccoli and Cauliflower Crunch Salad

Prep Time: 10 minutes

Cook Time: 0–2 minutes (optional light steaming)

Servings: 2–3

Ingredients:

1 cup broccoli florets (raw or lightly steamed)

1 cup cauliflower florets (raw or lightly steamed)

1/4 cup raisins (unsweetened)

2 tablespoons raw sunflower seeds

Zest of 1 lemon

1 tablespoon fresh lemon juice

1 tablespoon extra-virgin olive oil

Sea salt and black pepper, to taste

Optional: 1 tablespoon chopped fresh parsley or mint

1. If desired, steam broccoli and cauliflower for 1–2 minutes until just tender-crisp, then cool immediately in cold water to preserve crunch and nutrients.

2. In a large bowl, combine broccoli, cauliflower, raisins, and sunflower seeds.

3. In a small bowl, whisk together lemon zest, lemon juice, olive oil, salt, and pepper.

4. Pour the dressing over the vegetables and toss to coat.

5. Garnish with herbs if using. Serve immediately or refrigerate for up to 24 hours.

Optional Boost: Add a tablespoon of hemp seeds or chopped walnuts.

Lemon-Tahini Dressing

Prep Time: 5 minutes

Servings: Makes about 1/2 cup (4–6 servings)

Ingredients:

1/4 cup tahini (stirred if separated)

2–3 tablespoons fresh lemon juice (about 1 small lemon)

1 clove garlic, finely minced or grated

2–4 tablespoons water

Sea salt, to taste (start with 1/8 teaspoon)

1. In a small bowl or jar, whisk together tahini, lemon juice, and garlic. It may thicken initially.

2. Slowly whisk in water, one tablespoon at a time, until smooth and pourable.

3. Add sea salt to taste and stir to combine.

4. Store in the fridge for up to 5 days in a sealed container.

Optional Boost: Add a pinch of ground cumin or turmeric.

ANDREA D. RATLIFF

Olive Oil & Apple Cider Vinaigrette

Prep Time: 5 minutes

Servings: Makes about 1/2 cup (4–6 servings)

Ingredients:

1/4 cup extra virgin olive oil

2 tablespoons apple cider vinegar (with the mother)

1 teaspoon Dijon mustard

1–2 teaspoons pure maple syrup (to taste)

Pinch of sea salt and freshly ground black pepper

1. In a small bowl or jar, whisk or shake together all ingredients until emulsified.

2. Taste and adjust sweetness, acidity, or seasoning if desired.

3. Store in an airtight jar in the refrigerator for up to 5 days. Shake well before each use.

Serving Suggestion: Drizzle over mixed greens, roasted vegetables, or a quinoa salad.

Turmeric-Ginger Dressing

Prep Time: 5 minutes

Servings: Makes about 1/2 cup (4–6 servings)

Ingredients:

1/4 cup extra virgin olive oil

1 tablespoon fresh lemon juice (about 1/2 lemon)

1 teaspoon freshly grated ginger

1/2 teaspoon ground turmeric or 1 teaspoon freshly grated

1/8 teaspoon freshly ground black pepper

Optional: 1/2 teaspoon raw honey or maple syrup for balance

1. In a small bowl or jar, whisk together all ingredients until emulsified.

2. Taste and adjust seasoning (add more lemon or a touch of sweetener if desired).

3. Store in a sealed container in the refrigerator for up to 5 days. Shake well before each use.

Serving Suggestions: Drizzle over leafy greens, grain bowls, roasted veggies, or use as a dip for raw vegetables.

ANDREA D. RATLIFF

Avocado-Cilantro Lime Dressing

Prep Time: 5–10 minutes

Servings: Makes about 3/4 cup (enough for 4–6 salads)

Ingredients:

1 ripe avocado, peeled and pitted

1/4 cup fresh cilantro leaves (packed)

2 tablespoons fresh lime juice (about 1 lime)

2 tablespoons extra virgin olive oil

1 small garlic clove, minced

2–4 tablespoons water

Sea salt and freshly ground black pepper, to taste

1. In a blender or food processor, combine avocado, cilantro, lime juice, olive oil, and garlic.

2. Blend until smooth, adding water a tablespoon at a time to reach your preferred texture.

3. Season with salt and pepper to taste.

4. Use, or store in an airtight container in the fridge for up to 2 days.

Optional Boost: Add a pinch of ground cumin or jalapeño.

Miso-Ginger Dressing

Prep Time: 5 minutes

Servings: Makes about 4 servings (1/4 cup each)

Ingredients:

2 tablespoons white miso paste

2 tablespoons rice vinegar

1 tablespoon toasted sesame oil

1 tablespoon water

1 teaspoon freshly grated ginger

1 small garlic clove, finely grated or minced

Optional: 1 teaspoon maple syrup for balance (if desired)

1. In a small bowl or jar, whisk together all ingredients until smooth and well combined.

2. Add more water 1 teaspoon at a time for a thinner texture if needed.

3. Taste and adjust flavor to your preference—more vinegar for tang, more miso for saltiness.

4. Store in an airtight container in the fridge for up to 5 days.

Serving Ideas: Drizzle over mixed greens, grain bowls, steamed veggies, or roasted sweet potatoes.

ANDREA D. RATLIFF

Main Dishes

Baked Salmon with Lemon and Dill

Prep Time: 10 minutes

Cook Time: 15–20 minutes

Servings: 2)

Ingredients:

2 salmon fillets (about 5–6 oz each)

1 tablespoon extra-virgin olive oil

Juice of 1/2 lemon + 2–3 lemon slices

2 tablespoons fresh dill or 1 teaspoon dried dill

1 garlic clove, minced

Sea salt and black pepper, to taste

Optional side: 1–2 cups of mixed veggies (e.g., broccoli, carrots, zucchini), tossed in olive oil and roasted

1. Preheat oven to 400°F (200°C).
2. Place salmon fillets on a parchment-lined baking sheet.
3. Drizzle with olive oil and lemon juice. Sprinkle with dill, garlic, salt, and pepper.
4. Top with lemon slices.
5. Bake for 15–20 minutes, or until salmon flakes easily with a fork.
6. If roasting veggies, toss them in olive oil, salt, and pepper and roast on a separate sheet for 20–25 minutes.
7. Serve salmon with a side of roasted veggies.

Optional Boost: Add a sprinkle of turmeric to the veggie mix.

Chickpea and Spinach Coconut Curry

Prep Time: 10 minutes

Cook Time: 20 minutes

Servings: 4

Ingredients:

1 tablespoon extra-virgin olive oil or avocado oil

1 small onion, finely chopped

2 garlic cloves, minced

1 tablespoon freshly grated ginger or 1 tsp ground

1 teaspoon ground turmeric

1/2 teaspoon ground cumin

1/4 teaspoon ground black pepper

1 (15 oz) can chickpeas, drained and rinsed

1 (14 oz) can full-fat coconut milk

2 cups fresh baby spinach or 1 cup frozen

Sea salt, to taste

Juice of 1/2 lemon

Fresh cilantro for garnish

1. Heat oil in a large skillet or saucepan over medium heat. Add onions and sauté for 3–4 minutes until soft.

2. Stir in garlic, ginger, turmeric, cumin, and black pepper. Cook for 1 minute until fragrant.

3. Add chickpeas and stir to coat in the spices.

4. Pour in the coconut milk and bring to a gentle simmer.

5. Reduce heat and simmer for 10–15 minutes, stirring occasionally, until sauce thickens slightly.

6. Stir in spinach and cook just until wilted (1–2 minutes).

7. Add salt to taste and a squeeze of lemon juice, if using.

8. Garnish with fresh cilantro and serve warm.

Serving Suggestions: Serve over cooked quinoa, brown rice, or with warm whole grain flatbread.

Grilled Chicken with Quinoa and Roasted Broccoli

Prep Time: 10–15 minutes

Cook Time: 25–30 minutes

Servings: 2

Ingredients:

For the Chicken

2 skinless, boneless chicken breasts

1 tablespoon olive oil

1 teaspoon garlic powder

1/2 teaspoon turmeric

Sea salt and black pepper, to taste

Juice of 1/2 lemon

For the Quinoa

1/2 cup uncooked quinoa, rinsed

1 cup water or low-sodium vegetable broth

Pinch of sea salt

For the Roasted Broccoli

2 cups broccoli florets

1 tablespoon olive oil

1/2 teaspoon smoked paprika

Sea salt and black pepper, to taste

1. Cook the Quinoa

Combine quinoa, water (or broth), and a pinch of salt in a saucepan.

Bring to a boil, then reduce heat to low, cover, and simmer for 15 minutes or until water is absorbed.

Fluff with a fork and set aside.

2. Roast the Broccoli

Preheat oven to 400°F (200°C).

Toss broccoli florets with olive oil, paprika, salt, and pepper.

Spread on a baking sheet and roast for 20–25 minutes, until edges are crisp and golden.

3. Grill the Chicken

Rub chicken breasts with olive oil, garlic powder, turmeric, salt, pepper, and lemon juice.

Grill on a stovetop grill pan or outdoor grill over medium-high heat for about 5–6 minutes per side, or until cooked through and juices run clear.

4. Assemble

Plate grilled chicken alongside quinoa and roasted broccoli.

Garnish with fresh herbs like parsley or basil if desired.

Optional Boost: Add a drizzle of tahini or lemon-turmeric dressing.

Sweet Potato and Black Bean Tacos

Prep Time: 10 minutes

Cook Time: 25–30 minutes

Servings: 4 (makes about 8 small tacos)

Ingredients:

For the tacos:

2 medium sweet potatoes, peeled and diced

1 tablespoon extra-virgin olive oil

1/2 teaspoon ground cumin

1/2 teaspoon smoked paprika

1/4 teaspoon sea salt

1 (15 oz) can black beans, drained and rinsed

8 small corn or whole grain tortillas (gluten-free if needed)

For the avocado salsa:

1 ripe avocado, diced

1/4 cup red onion, finely chopped

1/2 cup cherry tomatoes, halved

Juice of 1 lime

1 tablespoon chopped cilantro

Pinch of sea salt

1. Roast the sweet potatoes:

Preheat oven to 400°F (200°C).

Toss diced sweet potatoes with olive oil, cumin, paprika, and salt.

Spread on a baking sheet and roast for 20–25 minutes, flipping halfway, until tender and slightly crisp.

2. In a small bowl, combine diced avocado, onion, cherry tomatoes, lime juice, cilantro, and salt. Mix gently.

3. Heat tortillas in a dry skillet or wrap in foil and warm in the oven for 5 minutes.

4. Assemble tacos:

Layer roasted sweet potatoes and black beans onto each tortilla.

Top with a generous spoonful of avocado salsa.

Serve.

Optional Boost: Add shredded red cabbage or a drizzle of tahini.

Stuffed Bell Peppers with Lentils and Brown Rice

Prep Time: 15 minutes

Cook Time: 35–40 minutes

Servings: 4

Ingredients:

4 large bell peppers (any color), tops cut off and seeds removed

1 tablespoon olive oil

1 small onion, finely chopped

2 garlic cloves, minced

1 cup cooked lentils (brown or green)

1 cup cooked brown rice

1/2 cup diced tomatoes (no-salt-added, fresh or canned)

1 teaspoon ground cumin

1/2 teaspoon smoked paprika

Sea salt and black pepper, to taste

2 tablespoons chopped parsley or cilantro

1 tablespoon ground flaxseed

1. Preheat oven to 375°F (190°C).

2. In a skillet, heat olive oil over medium heat. Sauté onion and garlic for 3–4 minutes until soft and fragrant.

3. Add cooked lentils, brown rice, diced tomatoes, cumin, paprika, salt, and pepper. Stir to combine and heat through. Mix in ground flaxseed if using.

4. Stuff each bell pepper with the lentil-rice mixture and place them in a baking dish.

5. Add a splash of water to the bottom of the dish to keep the peppers moist.

6. Cover with foil and bake for 30 minutes. Remove foil and bake an additional 5–10 minutes until peppers are tender.

7. Garnish with fresh parsley or cilantro before serving.

Optional Boost: Top with a spoonful of plain Greek yogurt or a drizzle of tahini.

ANDREA D. RATLIFF

Zucchini Noodles with Pesto and Cherry Tomatoes

Prep Time: 10 minutes

Cook Time: 3–5 minutes

Servings: 2

Ingredients:

For the noodles:

2 medium zucchinis, spiralized

1 cup cherry tomatoes, halved

1 tablespoon extra-virgin olive oil

Pinch of sea salt and black pepper

For the pesto:

1 cup fresh basil leaves

1/4 cup raw walnuts or pine nuts

1 small garlic clove

2 tablespoons nutritional yeast

1/4 cup extra virgin olive oil

Juice of 1/2 lemon

Sea salt, to taste

1. Add basil, nuts, garlic, lemon juice, and nutritional yeast (if using) to a food processor. Pulse until chopped. Slowly add olive oil while blending until smooth. Season with salt to taste.

2. Heat olive oil in a large skillet over medium heat. Add zucchini noodles and sauté for 2–3 minutes until just tender.

3. Add cherry tomatoes and cook for 1–2 minutes until warmed but not mushy.

4. Turn off heat and toss with 3–4 tablespoons of the pesto or to taste.

5. Divide into bowls and serve.

Optional Boost: Top with hemp seeds, microgreens, or crushed red pepper flakes.

Grilled Mackerel with Avocado Slaw

Prep Time: 10–15 minutes

Cook Time: 8–10 minutes

Servings: 2

Ingredients:

For the Mackerel

2 fresh mackerel fillets (skin on, about 4–5 oz each)

1 tablespoon olive oil

Juice of 1/2 lemon

1/2 teaspoon ground turmeric

1/4 teaspoon sea salt

Freshly ground black pepper, to taste

For the Avocado Slaw

2 cups shredded cabbage (green or purple)

1 ripe avocado, diced

1 tablespoon fresh lime juice

1 tablespoon extra-virgin olive oil

1 tablespoon chopped fresh cilantro

Sea salt and pepper to taste

1. In a small bowl, mix olive oil, lemon juice, turmeric, salt, and pepper. Brush mixture over the mackerel fillets.

2. Preheat grill or grill pan over medium-high heat. Grill mackerel skin-side down for about 4–5 minutes, then flip and grill for another 3–4 minutes, until cooked through and flakes easily.

3. In a large bowl, combine cabbage, avocado, lime juice, olive oil, and cilantro. Toss gently to coat. Season with salt and pepper to taste.

4. Plate the grilled mackerel alongside a generous serving of slaw.

5. Serve with an optional lemon wedge.

Optional Boost: Add a pinch of cumin or ground ginger to the slaw.

Wild-Caught Shrimp Stir-Fry with Bok Choy and Ginger

Prep Time: 10 minutes

Cook Time: 10 minutes

Servings: 2

Ingredients:

1/2 lb (about 225g) wild-caught shrimp, peeled and deveined

1 tablespoon avocado oil or extra virgin olive oil

2 cloves garlic, minced

1 tablespoon fresh ginger, grated

3 cups bok choy, chopped (including stems and leaves)

1 tablespoon low-sodium tamari or coconut aminos

1 teaspoon toasted sesame oil

Optional: sliced green onions or sesame seeds

Pinch of red pepper flakes

1. Heat avocado or olive oil in a large skillet or wok over medium-high heat.

2. Add garlic and ginger, sauté for 30 seconds until fragrant.

3. Add shrimp and cook for 2–3 minutes, flipping halfway, until pink and opaque.

4. Add chopped bok choy and tamari (or coconut aminos). Stir-fry for another 2–3 minutes, until the greens wilt and stems are slightly tender.

5. Drizzle with toasted sesame oil and remove from heat.

6. Garnish with green onions or sesame seeds if desired, and serve warm.

Optional Boost: Serve over cooked quinoa or cauliflower rice.

Turmeric Chicken and Vegetable Skillet

Prep Time: 10 minutes

Cook Time: 20–25 minutes

Servings: 4

Ingredients:

1 lb (450g) boneless, skinless chicken breast or thighs, cut into bite-sized pieces

2 tablespoons extra virgin olive oil or avocado oil

1 teaspoon ground turmeric

1/4 teaspoon ground black pepper

1/2 teaspoon sea salt or to taste

1/2 teaspoon smoked paprika (optional)

2 garlic cloves, minced

1 small red onion, sliced

1 red bell pepper, sliced

1 cup broccoli florets

1 cup sliced carrots

1 tablespoon lemon juice

Fresh parsley or cilantro, chopped

1. In a medium bowl, toss chicken with turmeric, black pepper, salt, and paprika (if using). Set aside.

2. Heat 1 tablespoon oil in a large skillet over medium heat. Add chicken and cook until golden and cooked through, about 6–8 minutes. Remove and set aside.

3. In the same skillet, add remaining oil and sauté garlic and onion for 2–3 minutes until softened.

4. Add bell pepper, carrots, and broccoli. Stir-fry for 5–7 minutes, until veggies are tender-crisp.

5. Return chicken to the skillet, stir to combine, and drizzle with lemon juice.

6. Cook for an additional 1–2 minutes until everything is well heated and coated.

7. Garnish with fresh herbs and serve hot.

Serving Tip: Enjoy on its own, or serve over a bed of quinoa or brown rice.

ANDREA D. RATLIFF

Eggplant and Mushroom Stir-Fry over Brown Rice

Prep Time: 10 minutes

Cook Time: 20 minutes

Servings: 2

Ingredients:

1 cup uncooked brown rice

2 tablespoons avocado oil or extra virgin olive oil

1 small eggplant, diced (about 2 cups)

1 cup mushrooms, sliced (shiitake, cremini, or button)

1/2 red bell pepper, sliced

2 garlic cloves, minced

1 tablespoon low-sodium tamari or coconut aminos (gluten-free option)

1/2 teaspoon ground ginger or 1 teaspoon fresh grated ginger

1/2 teaspoon turmeric powder

A pinch of black pepper

Chopped green onions or cilantro

1. Cook brown rice according to package instructions (about 2:1 water-to-rice ratio, simmer for \35–40 minutes). If pre-cooked or using instant, skip this step.

2. While rice cooks, heat oil in a large skillet or wok over medium heat.

3. Add garlic and ginger; sauté for 30 seconds until fragrant.

4. Add eggplant and stir-fry for 5–7 minutes until it begins to soften.

5. Add mushrooms and bell pepper; cook another 5–6 minutes, stirring occasionally.

6. Sprinkle in turmeric, black pepper, and tamari or coconut aminos. Stir well to coat veggies evenly.

7. Continue cooking for 2–3 more minutes, until veggies are tender but not mushy.

8. Serve the stir-fry over warm brown rice. Garnish with chopped green onions or cilantro if desired.

Optional Boost: Top with a tablespoon of hemp seeds or crushed walnuts.

Baked Tofu with Sweet Potato and Broccoli

Prep Time: 15 minutes

Cook Time: 30–35 minutes

Servings: 2–3

Ingredients:

For the bowl:

1 block (14 oz) extra-firm tofu, pressed and cubed

1 medium sweet potato, peeled and cubed

2 cups broccoli florets

1 tablespoon avocado oil or olive oil

1/2 teaspoon garlic powder

1/2 teaspoon smoked paprika (optional)

Sea salt and black pepper, to taste

For the tahini-ginger sauce:

2 tablespoons tahini

1 tablespoon fresh lemon juice

1 teaspoon grated fresh ginger or 1/2 tsp ground ginger

1–2 teaspoons maple syrup

1–2 tablespoons warm water (to thin the sauce)

Pinch of sea salt

1. Preheat oven to 400°F (200°C). Line a baking sheet with parchment paper.

2. In a large bowl, toss sweet potatoes and broccoli with 1/2 tablespoon oil, garlic powder, paprika, salt, and pepper. Spread on one side of the baking sheet.

3. In the same bowl, toss tofu cubes with the remaining oil and a pinch of salt. Spread on the other side of the sheet.

4. Bake for 30–35 minutes, flipping tofu and veggies halfway, until golden and tender.

5. While baking, whisk all tahini sauce ingredients in a small bowl. Adjust water for desired consistency.

6. Once everything is cooked, divide tofu, sweet potatoes, and broccoli into bowls.

7. Drizzle with tahini-ginger sauce and serve warm.

Optional Boost: Add a sprinkle of sesame seeds or chopped fresh cilantro.

ANDREA D. RATLIFF

Moroccan-Spiced Chicken Thighs with Roasted Carrots

Prep Time: 10 minutes

Cook Time: 30–35 minutes

Servings: 4

Ingredients:

For the Chicken

4 boneless, skinless chicken thighs

1 tablespoon olive oil

1 teaspoon ground cumin

1 teaspoon smoked paprika

1/2 teaspoon ground cinnamon

1/4 teaspoon ground turmeric (optional boost)

1/4 teaspoon black pepper

1/2 teaspoon sea salt

Juice of 1/2 lemon

For the Roasted Carrots

4–5 medium carrots, peeled and sliced into sticks

1 tablespoon olive oil

1/2 teaspoon ground cumin

1/2 teaspoon smoked paprika

Pinch of cinnamon

Sea salt and black pepper, to taste

1. Preheat oven to 400°F (200°C).

2. In a bowl, mix olive oil, spices, and lemon juice. Rub mixture over chicken thighs and let marinate while prepping the carrots (or up to 2 hours in the fridge).

3. Toss sliced carrots with olive oil, spices, salt, and pepper. Spread on a baking sheet.

4. Place the marinated chicken on a separate baking tray or next to the carrots if there's room.

5. Roast everything for 25–30 minutes, flipping carrots halfway through, until chicken is cooked through (165°F internal temp) and carrots are tender and slightly caramelized.

6. Let chicken rest for 5 minutes before serving.

Optional Boost: Garnish with chopped parsley or cilantro and serve with a side of quinoa or leafy greens.

Farro Bowl with Roasted Veggies and Lemon-Herb Dressing

Prep Time: 10–15 minutes

Cook Time: 25–30 minutes

Servings: 2–3

Ingredients:

For the bowl:

3/4 cup uncooked farro (rinsed)

2 cups water or low-sodium vegetable broth

1 cup chopped broccoli

1 red bell pepper, chopped

1 zucchini, sliced

1/2 red onion, sliced

1 tablespoon extra-virgin olive oil

Salt and pepper, to taste

For the lemon-herb dressing:

Juice of 1 lemon

2 tablespoons extra virgin olive oil

1 clove garlic, minced

1 tablespoon chopped fresh parsley or basil

1/2 teaspoon Dijon mustard

Salt and black pepper, to taste

1. In a pot, combine farro with water or broth. Bring to a boil, then reduce to a simmer and cook for 20–25 minutes, or until tender. Drain any excess liquid.

2. Roast the veggies:

Preheat oven to 400°F (200°C).

Spread broccoli, bell pepper, zucchini, and red onion on a baking sheet. Drizzle with olive oil and season with salt and pepper.

Roast for 20–25 minutes, flipping halfway, until tender and slightly golden.

3. Whisk together lemon juice, olive oil, garlic, parsley, Dijon, salt, and pepper in a small bowl.

4. Assemble the bowl:

Divide cooked farro into bowls. Top with roasted vegetables.

Drizzle with lemon-herb dressing. Serve warm or room temperature.

Optional Boost: Add a handful of arugula or microgreens on top

Miso-Glazed Cod with Steamed Greens and Brown Rice

Prep Time: 10 minutes

Cook Time: 15–20 minutes

Servings: 2

Ingredients:

For the cod:

2 cod fillets (about 5–6 oz each)

2 tablespoons white or yellow miso paste (fermented)

1 tablespoon rice vinegar or fresh lime juice

1 tablespoon pure maple syrup or honey

1 teaspoon grated fresh ginger

1 teaspoon toasted sesame oil

For the sides:

1 cup brown rice (cooked according to package instructions)

2 cups steamed greens (bok choy, kale, or spinach)

1 teaspoon olive oil or sesame oil (for drizzling)

Optional: sesame seeds or chopped scallions for garnish

1. Cook brown rice ahead of time or while the fish is baking.

2. In a small bowl, mix miso paste, vinegar, maple syrup, ginger, and sesame oil until smooth.

3. Preheat oven to 400°F (200°C). Line a baking sheet with parchment paper. Place cod fillets on the sheet and brush evenly with miso glaze.

4. Bake cod for 12–15 minutes, or until it flakes easily with a fork.

5. While cod is baking, steam greens in a steamer basket or sauté briefly in a pan with a splash of water until just wilted. Drizzle with a bit of olive or sesame oil.

6. Serve cod over brown rice with steamed greens on the side. Garnish with sesame seeds or scallions if desired.

Optional Boost: Add a squeeze of lemon or lime over the fish before serving.

Quinoa and Vegetable-Stuffed Portobello Mushrooms

Prep Time: 15 minutes

Cook Time: 25 minutes

Servings: 2 (makes 4 stuffed mushrooms)

Ingredients:

4 large Portobello mushroom caps (stems and gills removed)

1/2 cup uncooked quinoa (rinsed)

1 cup water or low-sodium vegetable broth

1 tablespoon extra-virgin olive oil

1/2 cup chopped zucchini

1/2 cup chopped red bell pepper

1 cup baby spinach

2 cloves garlic, minced

1/4 teaspoon dried thyme

Sea salt and black pepper, to taste

1 tablespoon ground flaxseed

Fresh parsley or basil for garnish (optional)

1. Preheat oven to 375°F (190°C). Line a baking sheet with parchment paper.

2. Place mushroom caps on the baking sheet, gill side up. Brush lightly with olive oil and sprinkle with salt. Bake for 10 minutes to soften.

3. Meanwhile, in a small saucepan, bring water or broth to a boil. Add quinoa, reduce heat, cover, and simmer for 15 minutes or until quinoa is tender and liquid is absorbed. Set aside.

4. In a skillet, heat 1 tablespoon olive oil over medium heat. Add garlic, zucchini, and bell pepper. Sauté for 3–4 minutes until softened.

5. Stir in spinach and cook until wilted. Add cooked quinoa, thyme, salt, pepper, and ground flaxseed (if using). Mix well.

6. Spoon the quinoa-veggie mixture into the pre-baked mushrooms.

7. Return to the oven and bake for another 10–12 minutes, until heated through and slightly golden on top.

8. Garnish with fresh parsley or basil and serve warm.

Optional Boost: Add a sprinkle of nutritional yeast or crumbled goat cheese (if tolerated)

Ground Turkey and Sweet Potato Skillet

Prep Time: 10 minutes

Cook Time: 20–25 minutes

Servings: 4

Ingredients:

1 tablespoon avocado oil or olive oil

1 lb ground turkey (preferably organic or pasture-raised)

2 medium sweet potatoes, peeled and diced

1 small red bell pepper, chopped

1 cup chopped spinach or kale

1 small red onion, diced

2 cloves garlic, minced

1/2 teaspoon ground turmeric

1/2 teaspoon smoked paprika

1/2 teaspoon ground cumin

Pinch of black pepper

Sea salt, to taste

Optional: chopped fresh parsley or cilantro

1. Heat oil in a large skillet over medium heat.

2. Add diced onion and cook for 2–3 minutes until softened.

3. Stir in garlic, sweet potatoes, turmeric, paprika, and cumin. Cook for 5–7 minutes, stirring occasionally.

4. Push veggies to the side of the skillet and add ground turkey. Break it up with a spatula and cook until browned and fully cooked, about 8–10 minutes.

5. Mix the turkey with the vegetables. Add bell pepper and spinach; cook for another 2–3 minutes until spinach wilts and everything is well combined.

6. Season with salt and black pepper to taste. Garnish with fresh herbs if desired.

7. Serve warm on its own or with a side of avocado or brown rice.

Optional Boost: Add a squeeze of fresh lime juice before serving.

Roasted Cauliflower Steaks with Herb Sauce

Prep Time: 10 minutes

Cook Time: 25–30 minutes

Servings: 2–3

Ingredients:

For the cauliflower steaks

1 large head of cauliflower

2 tablespoons extra virgin olive oil

1/2 teaspoon garlic powder

Sea salt and black pepper, to taste

For the herb sauce**:

1/2 cup fresh parsley (flat-leaf or curly), finely chopped

1 clove garlic, minced

Zest and juice of 1 lemon

2 tablespoons extra virgin olive oil

1/4 teaspoon sea salt

Optional: pinch of crushed red pepper flakes or black pepper

1. Prepare the cauliflower steaks:

Preheat oven to 425°F (220°C).

Remove outer leaves and trim the base of the cauliflower, keeping the core intact.

Slice into 3/4–1 inch thick "steaks" (you should get 2–3 from the center; save the smaller pieces for roasting alongside).

Place on a parchment-lined baking sheet. Brush both sides with olive oil and sprinkle with garlic powder, salt, and pepper.

2. Roast for 20–25 minutes, flipping halfway through, until golden and fork-tender.

3. While cauliflower roasts, whisk together parsley, garlic, lemon zest and juice, olive oil, salt, and red pepper flakes in a bowl.

4. Plate the cauliflower steaks and drizzle with herb sauce. Serve warm.

Optional Boost: Serve with a side of quinoa or lentils.

Mediterranean Baked Cod with Tomatoes and Olives

Prep Time: 10 minutes

Cook Time: 15–20 minutes

Servings: 2

Ingredients:

2 cod fillets (about 5–6 oz each)

1 cup cherry tomatoes, halved

1/4 cup Kalamata or green olives, sliced

2 tablespoons extra virgin olive oil

2 cloves garlic, minced

1/2 teaspoon dried oregano

1/2 teaspoon dried basil or Italian seasoning

Juice of half a lemon

Sea salt and black pepper, to taste

Fresh parsley, chopped

1. Preheat oven to 400°F (200°C).

2. Place cod fillets in a lightly greased baking dish.

3. In a bowl, mix cherry tomatoes, olives, olive oil, garlic, oregano, basil, lemon juice, salt, and pepper.

4. Spoon the tomato-olive mixture over the fish.

5. Bake uncovered for 15–20 minutes, or until the cod flakes easily with a fork.

6. Garnish with fresh parsley and serve warm.

Serving suggestion: Pair with quinoa, brown rice, or a leafy green salad.

Side Dishes

Roasted Brussels Sprouts with Balsamic Glaze

Prep Time: 10 minutes

Cook Time: 25–30 minutes

Servings: 4

Ingredients:

1 lb Brussels sprouts, trimmed and halved

2 tablespoons extra virgin olive oil

Sea salt and freshly ground black pepper, to taste

2 tablespoons balsamic vinegar

1 teaspoon pure maple syrup or raw honey

Optional: pinch of garlic powder or red pepper flakes for extra flavor

1. Preheat oven to 400°F (200°C).

2. In a bowl, toss Brussels sprouts with olive oil, salt, and pepper.

3. Spread them evenly on a baking sheet, cut side down.

4. Roast for 20–25 minutes, or until golden and crispy on the edges.

5. While roasting, make the glaze: in a small saucepan over low heat, combine balsamic vinegar and maple syrup (if using). Simmer until slightly thickened, about 3–5 minutes.

6. Remove Brussels sprouts from the oven and drizzle with balsamic glaze.

7. Toss gently and serve warm.

Optional Boost: Sprinkle with toasted walnuts or hemp seeds.

Garlic Sautéed Spinach

Prep Time: 5 minutes

Cook Time: 5 minutes

Servings: 2

Ingredients:

1 tablespoon extra-virgin olive oil

2–3 cloves garlic, thinly sliced or minced

4 cups fresh spinach or 1 bag pre-washed baby spinach

Pinch of sea salt

Cracked black pepper, to taste

Squeeze of fresh lemon juice

1. Heat olive oil in a large skillet over medium heat.

2. Add garlic and sauté for 30–60 seconds, just until fragrant (avoid browning).

3. Add spinach and toss gently with tongs until wilted, about 2–3 minutes.

4. Season with a pinch of sea salt and black pepper.

5. Remove from heat and finish with a squeeze of fresh lemon juice, if desired.

6. Serve as a side dish or over quinoa, brown rice, or toast.

Optional Boost: Sprinkle with hemp seeds or chopped almonds.

ANDREA D. RATLIFF

Quinoa with Lemon and Parsley

Prep Time: 5 minutes

Cook Time: 15 minutes

Servings: 2–3

Ingredients:

1 cup uncooked quinoa (rinsed)

2 cups water or low-sodium vegetable broth

2 tablespoons fresh lemon juice (plus more to taste)

1 teaspoon lemon zest

1/4 cup finely chopped fresh parsley

1 tablespoon extra-virgin olive oil

Sea salt and freshly ground black pepper, to taste

1. Rinse quinoa under cold water using a fine mesh strainer to remove bitterness.

2. In a medium saucepan, combine quinoa and water or broth. Bring to a boil, then reduce heat to low, cover, and simmer for 15 minutes, or until liquid is absorbed and quinoa is fluffy.

3. Remove from heat and let it sit, covered, for 5 minutes.

4. Fluff quinoa with a fork. Stir in lemon juice, lemon zest, olive oil, and chopped parsley.

5. Season with salt and pepper to taste.

6. Serve warm or chilled as a side dish or light lunch.

Optional Boost: Add chopped cucumber, cherry tomatoes, or a handful of chickpeas to turn it into a refreshing anti-inflammatory quinoa salad.

Turmeric Cauliflower Rice

Prep Time: 10 minutes

Cook Time: 5–7 minutes

Servings: 2–3

Ingredients:

1 medium head of cauliflower or 3–4 cups pre-riced cauliflower

1 tablespoon extra-virgin olive oil or avocado oil

1/2 teaspoon ground turmeric

A pinch of black pepper

1/4 teaspoon sea salt or to taste

1–2 cloves garlic, minced (optional)

1 tablespoon chopped fresh parsley or cilantro

Juice of 1/2 lemon

1. If starting with a whole cauliflower, cut it into florets and pulse in a food processor until it resembles rice. (Be careful not to over-process.)

2. In a large skillet, heat the oil over medium heat.

3. Add garlic (if using) and sauté for 30 seconds until fragrant.

4. Stir in the cauliflower rice, turmeric, black pepper, and salt.

5. Cook for 5–7 minutes, stirring occasionally, until the cauliflower is tender but not mushy.

6. Remove from heat and stir in lemon juice and fresh herbs if using.

7. Serve warm as a side dish or as a base for a veggie bowl or lean protein.

Optional Boost: Add a sprinkle of hemp seeds or toss in sautéed greens.

Cucumber and Avocado Salad

Prep Time: 10 minutes

Servings: 2

Ingredients:

1 large cucumber, thinly sliced (or halved and sliced)

1 ripe avocado, diced

1 tablespoon extra-virgin olive oil

Juice of 1 lime

1 tablespoon chopped fresh cilantro or parsley

Pinch of sea salt

Pinch of freshly ground black pepper

Optional: 1 tablespoon hemp seeds or pumpkin seeds

1. In a medium bowl, combine the cucumber slices and diced avocado.

2. In a small bowl, whisk together olive oil, lime juice, salt, and pepper.

3. Pour the dressing over the cucumber and avocado.

4. Gently toss to coat evenly without mashing the avocado.

5. Garnish with chopped herbs and optional seeds.

6. Serve, or chill briefly before serving for enhanced flavor.

Optional Boost: Add a few thin slices of red onion or radish.

Roasted Carrots with Cumin and Coriander

Prep Time: 10 minutes

Cook Time: 25–30 minutes

Servings: 4

Ingredients:

1 lb (about 6–8 medium) carrots, peeled and cut into sticks or rounds

1 tablespoon extra-virgin olive oil

1 teaspoon ground cumin

1/2 teaspoon ground coriander

1/4 teaspoon sea salt

1/8 teaspoon black pepper

Optional: chopped fresh parsley or cilantro for garnish

1. Preheat oven to 400°F (200°C).

2. In a large mixing bowl, toss carrots with olive oil, cumin, coriander, salt, and pepper until evenly coated.

3. Spread carrots in a single layer on a parchment-lined baking sheet.

4. Roast for 25–30 minutes, flipping halfway through, until tender and lightly browned.

5. Transfer to a serving dish and garnish with fresh herbs if desired.

Optional Boost: Add a squeeze of fresh lemon juice before serving.

Mashed Sweet Potatoes with Olive Oil

Prep Time: 10 minutes

Cook Time: 20–25 minutes

Servings: 2–3

Ingredients:

2 medium sweet potatoes, peeled and cubed

1–2 tablespoons extra virgin olive oil

1/2 teaspoon ground cinnamon

Sea salt, to taste

Freshly ground black pepper, to taste

Optional: A squeeze of fresh lemon juice or chopped fresh herbs (parsley or rosemary)

1. Place cubed sweet potatoes in a saucepan and cover with water.

2. Bring to a boil over medium-high heat, then reduce heat and simmer for 15–20 minutes, or until tender when pierced with a fork.

3. Drain and return the sweet potatoes to the pot.

4. Add olive oil, sea salt, pepper, and cinnamon (if using).

5. Mash with a fork or potato masher until smooth and creamy. For an extra silky texture, use an immersion blender.

6. Taste and adjust seasoning. Garnish with fresh herbs or a light drizzle of olive oil if desired.

7. Serve warm.

Optional Boost: Stir in a spoonful of ground flaxseed or hemp seeds.

Red Cabbage Slaw with Apple Cider Vinaigrette

Prep Time: 10 minutes

Servings: 4

Ingredients:

For the slaw:

3 cups shredded red cabbage

1 medium carrot, julienned or grated

1 small green apple, thinly sliced or matchstick-cut

2 tablespoons chopped fresh parsley or cilantro (optional)

1 tablespoon raw sunflower or pumpkin seeds

For the vinaigrette**:

2 tablespoons apple cider vinegar (with "the mother")

2 tablespoons extra virgin olive oil

1 teaspoon Dijon mustard

1 teaspoon pure maple syrup or raw honey

Pinch of sea salt

Freshly ground black pepper, to taste

1. In a large bowl, combine shredded cabbage, carrot, apple, and herbs/seeds if using.

2. In a small bowl or jar, whisk together apple cider vinegar, olive oil, Dijon mustard, maple syrup, salt, and pepper until well blended.

3. Pour the vinaigrette over the slaw and toss well to coat evenly.

4. Let the slaw sit for at least 10 minutes before serving to allow flavors to meld.

Optional Boost: Add a teaspoon of ground flaxseed or sprinkle hemp seeds on top for omega-3s.

ANDREA D. RATLIFF

Steamed Broccoli with Lemon and Pumpkin Seeds

Prep Time: 5 minutes

Cook Time: 5–7 minutes

Servings: 2

Ingredients:

2 cups broccoli florets (fresh or frozen)

1 tablespoon fresh lemon juice

2 tablespoons raw or dry-roasted pumpkin seeds (pepitas)

1 teaspoon extra virgin olive oil

Sea salt and freshly ground black pepper, to taste

Lemon zest

1. Steam broccoli in a steamer basket over boiling water for 5–7 minutes, until bright green and tender-crisp.

2. Transfer to a bowl and drizzle with lemon juice and olive oil (if using).

3. Sprinkle with pumpkin seeds, a pinch of salt, and black pepper to taste.

4. Add lemon zest on top for extra flavor, if desired.

5. Serve warm as a side or a light snack.

Optional Boost: Add a pinch of chili flakes or turmeric.

Grilled Zucchini with Fresh Herbs

Prep Time: 5–10 minutes

Cook Time: 5–7 minutes

Servings: 2–3

Ingredients:

2 medium zucchinis, sliced into 1/4-inch rounds or long strips

1 tablespoon extra-virgin olive oil

1/2 teaspoon sea salt

1/4 teaspoon black pepper

1 tablespoon chopped fresh herbs (such as basil, oregano, thyme, or a mix)

Optional: squeeze of fresh lemon juice or zest

1. Preheat a grill or grill pan over medium-high heat.

2. In a bowl, toss zucchini slices with olive oil, salt, and pepper.

3. Grill zucchini for 2–3 minutes on each side, until tender and grill-marked.

4. Remove from heat and sprinkle immediately with fresh herbs.

5. Optional: finish with a squeeze of lemon juice or a pinch of lemon zest before serving.

Optional Boost: Add a few grilled cherry tomatoes or a drizzle of balsamic glaze.

ANDREA D. RATLIFF

Snacks

Fresh Berries with a Handful of Walnuts

Prep Time: 2–3 minutes

Servings: 2

Ingredients:

1 cup fresh mixed berries (blueberries, raspberries, blackberries, strawberries)

1/4 cup raw or lightly toasted walnuts

1. Rinse the berries under cool water and gently pat them dry.

2. Divide berries into two small bowls.

3. Sprinkle a generous handful (about 2 tablespoons) of walnuts on each bowl.

4. Serve as a snack, breakfast side, or dessert.

Optional Boost:

Add a dollop of plain Greek yogurt for probiotics.

Sprinkle with a pinch of ground cinnamon.

Apple Slices with Almond Butter

Prep Time: 3–5 minutes

Servings: 2

Ingredients:

1 large apple (any variety, preferably organic), cored and sliced

2 tablespoons unsweetened almond butter

Optional toppings:

A sprinkle of ground cinnamon

A few crushed walnuts or chia seeds

A drizzle of raw honey

1. Wash, core, and slice the apple into wedges or rounds.

2. Spread about 1 tablespoon of almond butter over each serving of apple slices.

3. Sprinkle with cinnamon, chia seeds, or crushed nuts if desired.

4. Serve as a snack or light breakfast.

Optional Boost: Serve with a warm cup of green tea.

Hummus with Carrot and Cucumber Sticks

Prep Time: 10 minutes

Servings: 4 snack portions

Ingredients:

For the Hummus:

1 can (15 oz) chickpeas, drained and rinsed (or 1.5 cups cooked)

2 tablespoons tahini

2 tablespoons fresh lemon juice

1–2 tablespoons extra virgin olive oil

1 garlic clove (optional)

1/2 teaspoon ground cumin (optional)

2–3 tablespoons water

Sea salt, to taste

For the Veggies:

2 medium carrots, peeled and cut into sticks

1 medium cucumber, sliced into sticks or rounds

1. Make the Hummus:

In a food processor or blender, combine chickpeas, tahini, lemon juice, olive oil, garlic (if using), cumin, and a pinch of salt.

Blend until smooth, adding water gradually until the hummus reaches your desired texture.

2. While blending, cut carrots and cucumber into sticks for dipping.

3. Spoon hummus into a bowl and drizzle with a little olive oil. Serve with fresh veggie sticks.

Optional Boost: Sprinkle hummus with paprika or hemp seeds

ANDREA D. RATLIFF

Chia Pudding with Cinnamon and Berries

Prep Time: 5 minutes

Chill Time: 2 hours or overnight

Servings: 2

Ingredients:

1/4 cup chia seeds

1 cup unsweetened almond milk

1/2 teaspoon ground cinnamon

1/2 teaspoon vanilla extract

1–2 teaspoons pure maple syrup or raw honey

1/2 cup mixed berries (blueberries, raspberries, strawberries)

1. In a bowl or jar, combine chia seeds, almond milk, cinnamon, vanilla extract, and maple syrup.

2. Stir thoroughly to avoid clumping. Let sit for 5 minutes, then stir again.

3. Cover and refrigerate for at least 2 hours or overnight until it thickens to a pudding-like consistency.

4. When ready to serve, stir once more and divide into two bowls or jars.

5. Top with fresh berries and enjoy.

Optional Boost: Sprinkle with hemp seeds or a few crushed walnuts.

Handful of Pumpkin Seeds or Sunflower Seeds

Prep Time: 1 minute

Servings: 1

Ingredients:

1/4 cup raw or dry-roasted pumpkin seeds or sunflower seeds (unsalted, no added oils)

Optional:

A pinch of sea salt

A dash of smoked paprika, turmeric, or cinnamon

1. Measure out a small handful (about 1/4 cup) of pumpkin or sunflower seeds.

2. Eat as-is, or toss with your choice of spices for added flavor.

3. Optional toasting: Lightly toast seeds in a dry skillet over medium heat for 3–4 minutes, stirring frequently, until fragrant and slightly golden.

Optional Boost: Mix with a few dried, unsweetened tart cherries or goji berries.

Avocado on Whole Grain or Gluten-Free Crackers

Prep Time: 5 minutes

Servings: 2

Ingredients:

1 ripe avocado

6–8 whole grain or gluten-free crackers (look for ones with minimal ingredients and no added sugar or oils)

Squeeze of fresh lemon or lime juice (optional)

Pinch of sea salt

Pinch of black pepper

Optional toppings:

Red pepper flakes

Hemp seeds or chia seeds

Microgreens or arugula

Sliced cherry tomatoes

1. Cut avocado in half, remove the pit, and scoop the flesh into a bowl.

2. Mash the avocado with a fork. Add lemon juice, salt, and pepper to taste.

3. Spread the mashed avocado onto crackers.

4. Add optional toppings for extra nutrients and texture.

5. Serve as a snack or light meal.

Optional Boost: Add a sprinkle of turmeric with black pepper or a drizzle of extra virgin olive oil

Greek Yogurt with Turmeric and Honey (or Cinnamon)

Prep Time: 3–5 minutes

Servings: 1–2

Ingredients:

1 cup plain, unsweetened Greek yogurt (with live active cultures)

1/4 teaspoon ground turmeric

1/8 teaspoon ground black pepper

1/2–1 teaspoon raw honey or ground cinnamon

Optional: a pinch of ground ginger or cardamom

Optional toppings: crushed walnuts, chia seeds, or a few fresh berries

1. In a bowl, combine Greek yogurt, turmeric, and honey (or cinnamon). Stir until smooth and evenly colored.

2. If using black pepper or other spices, mix them in as well.

3. Top with optional additions like nuts, seeds, or berries for extra texture and nutrients.

4. Serve as a snack or breakfast.

Optional Boost: Let the mixture sit for a few minutes before eating to allow the turmeric flavor to mellow slightly.

Roasted Chickpeas with Sea Salt and Paprika

Prep Time: 5–10 minutes

Cook Time: 30–40 minutes

Servings: 2–4 (makes about 1.5 cups)

Ingredients:

1 can (15 oz) chickpeas (garbanzo beans), drained and rinsed

1 tablespoon extra-virgin olive oil

1/2 teaspoon sea salt

1 teaspoon smoked or sweet paprika

Optional: pinch of cayenne pepper for heat, or 1/4 teaspoon turmeric

1. Preheat oven to 400°F (200°C).

2. Pat chickpeas very dry with a clean towel—this helps them get crispy.

3. Spread chickpeas on a baking sheet lined with parchment paper.

4. Drizzle with olive oil and sprinkle with sea salt, paprika, and any optional spices.

5. Toss until evenly coated and spread them into a single layer.

6. Roast for 30–40 minutes, shaking the pan halfway through, until chickpeas are golden and crispy.

7. Let cool slightly before serving. They will continue to crisp up as they cool.

Storage Tip: Store in an airtight container at room temperature for up to 2 days (they're best fresh).

Edamame with a Dash of Sea Salt

Prep Time: 2 minutes

Cook Time: 5–7 minutes (if using frozen)

Servings: 2

Ingredients:

2 cups frozen edamame in pods or shelled

Water, for boiling or steaming

1/4 teaspoon sea salt (or to taste)

1. Bring a small pot of water to a boil.

2. Add frozen edamame and cook for 5–6 minutes until tender and heated through. (Alternatively, steam for 5 minutes.)

3. Drain and transfer to a serving bowl.

4. Sprinkle lightly with sea salt. Toss and serve warm.

Optional Boost: Add a sprinkle of chili flakes, sesame seeds, or a squeeze of fresh lemon juice

Smoothie Pops (Banana, Berries, and Spinach)

Prep Time: 10 minutes

Freeze Time: 4–6 hours (or overnight)

Servings: Makes about 6 popsicles

Ingredients:

2 medium zucchinis, sliced into 1 ripe banana

1 cup fresh or frozen mixed berries (blueberries, raspberries, strawberries)

1 cup fresh spinach (lightly packed)

1/2 cup unsweetened almond milk or coconut water

1 tablespoon ground flaxseed or chia seeds

1–2 teaspoons pure maple syrup or raw honey

1/2 teaspoon vanilla extract

1. Add banana, berries, spinach, almond milk, flaxseed (or chia seeds), and sweetener (if using) to a blender.

2. Blend until completely smooth.

3. Taste and adjust sweetness as needed.

4. Pour the smoothie mixture into popsicle molds.

5. Insert sticks and freeze for 4–6 hours or until solid.

6. To release, run molds under warm water for a few seconds and gently pull out the pops.

Optional Boost: Add a scoop of plain Greek yogurt or protein powder.

Desserts

ANDREA D. RATLIFF

Dark Chocolate-Dipped Strawberries

Prep Time: 10 minutes

Servings: 4 (makes about 12 dipped strawberries)

Ingredients:

12 large fresh strawberries (washed and thoroughly dried)

1/2 cup dark chocolate chips or chopped dark chocolate (70% cocoa or higher)

1/2 teaspoon coconut oil

Optional toppings:

Crushed walnuts or pistachios

Shredded unsweetened coconut

A light sprinkle of flaky sea salt

1. Place the dark chocolate and coconut oil (if using) in a small heat-safe bowl.

2. Melt the chocolate using a double boiler or microwave in 20–30 second intervals, stirring until smooth.

3. Hold each strawberry by the stem and dip into the melted chocolate, covering about 3/4 of the berry.

4. Gently twist and let the excess chocolate drip off.

5. Place dipped strawberries on a parchment-lined tray.

6. If using toppings, sprinkle them over the chocolate before it sets.

7. Refrigerate for 10–15 minutes or until chocolate is firm.

8. Serve chilled or at room temperature.

Optional Boost: Drizzle with a tiny bit of almond butter before chilling.

Chia Seed Pudding with Berries and Cinnamon

Prep Time: 5 minutes

Chill Time: 2–4 hours or overnight

Servings: 2

Ingredients:

1/4 cup chia seeds

1 cup unsweetened almond milk

1/2 teaspoon ground cinnamon

1 teaspoon pure vanilla extract

1–2 teaspoons pure maple syrup or raw honey

1/2 cup mixed berries (blueberries, raspberries, strawberries)

Optional: 1 tablespoon ground flaxseed or hemp hearts

1. In a mixing bowl or jar, combine chia seeds, almond milk, cinnamon, vanilla (if using), and maple syrup.

2. Stir well to prevent clumping. Let sit for 10 minutes, then stir again.

3. Cover and refrigerate for at least 2 hours or overnight until it thickens into a pudding-like texture.

4. Before serving, give it a good stir and top with fresh or thawed berries.

5. Sprinkle with ground flaxseed or hemp hearts if desired.

Optional Boost: Add a few crushed walnuts or a spoonful of almond butter.

ANDREA D. RATLIFF

Baked Apples with Walnuts and a Drizzle of Maple Syrup

Prep Time: 10 minutes

Cook Time: 25–30 minutes

Servings: 2

Ingredients:

2 medium apples (such as Honeycrisp, Fuji, or Gala), cored

1/4 cup chopped walnuts

1/2 teaspoon ground cinnamon

1 tablespoon pure maple syrup

1 teaspoon coconut oil or avocado oil

Pinch of sea salt

Optional garnish: plain Greek yogurt or dairy-free yogurt

1. Preheat oven to 375°F (190°C).

2. In a small bowl, mix walnuts, cinnamon, sea salt, and coconut oil (if using).

3. Stuff the walnut mixture into the cored center of each apple.

4. Place apples in a small baking dish and drizzle with maple syrup.

5. Add a splash of water (2–3 tablespoons) to the bottom of the dish to prevent sticking.

6. Cover with foil and bake for 20 minutes, then uncover and bake an additional 5–10 minutes, until apples are soft and golden.

7. Let cool slightly. Serve warm, optionally topped with a dollop of yogurt.

Optional Boost: Sprinkle with ground flaxseed before serving.

Avocado Chocolate Mousse

Prep Time: 5–10 minutes

Servings: 2

Ingredients:

2 ripe avocados

1/4 cup unsweetened cocoa powder

2–3 tablespoons pure maple syrup or raw honey (adjust to taste)

1/4 cup unsweetened almond milk

1 teaspoon vanilla extract

Pinch of sea salt

Optional: 1/4 teaspoon ground cinnamon or a dash of espresso powder

1. Scoop the avocado flesh into a food processor or high-speed blender.

2. Add cocoa powder, maple syrup, almond milk, vanilla extract, salt, and any optional spices.

3. Blend until completely smooth and creamy. Scrape down sides as needed.

4. Taste and adjust sweetness or cocoa for desired richness.

5. Spoon into serving dishes, or chill for 30 minutes for a firmer texture.

Optional Toppings:

Fresh berries (like raspberries or strawberries)

A sprinkle of crushed walnuts or cacao nibs

A dollop of coconut whipped cream

Banana Nice Cream

Prep Time: 5 minutes (plus freezing time)

Servings: 2

Ingredients:

2 ripe bananas, peeled, sliced, and frozen overnight

1/2 teaspoon ground cinnamon

1/4 teaspoon pure vanilla extract (optional)

1/4 cup frozen berries

Splash of unsweetened almond milk (if needed, for blending)

1. Place the frozen banana slices in a high-speed blender or food processor.

2. Blend until smooth and creamy, stopping to scrape down the sides as needed. Add a splash of almond milk only if needed to help it blend.

3. Once smooth, add cinnamon and vanilla extract. Blend again briefly to combine.

4. (Optional) Pulse in frozen berries for a fruity twist or stir them in for a chunky texture.

5. Serve right away for soft-serve texture, or freeze for 1–2 hours for a firmer scoopable consistency.

Optional Boost: Sprinkle with chopped walnuts or a drizzle of almond butter

Coconut Yogurt Parfait with Almonds and Blueberries

Prep Time: 5 minutes

Servings: 2

Ingredients:

1 cup unsweetened coconut yogurt (with live active cultures)

1/2 cup fresh or frozen blueberries

1/4 cup sliced or chopped raw almonds

1 tablespoon chia seeds or ground flaxseed (optional)

1–2 teaspoons pure maple syrup or raw honey (optional)

A pinch of cinnamon or nutmeg

1. In two small glasses or bowls, layer 1/4 cup of coconut yogurt in each.

2. Add a layer of blueberries, then sprinkle with almonds.

3. Repeat the layers with the remaining yogurt and toppings.

4. Drizzle with maple syrup or honey if desired.

5. Sprinkle with chia seeds and a pinch of cinnamon or nutmeg.

6. Serve or chill for up to 24 hours.

Optional Boost: Add a few spoonfuls of unsweetened granola or hemp hearts.

ANDREA D. RATLIFF

Almond Flour Brownies (Naturally Sweetened)

Prep Time: 10 minutes

Cook Time: 25–30 minutes

Servings: 9 brownies

Ingredients:

2 medium zucchinis, sliced into 1 ripe banana

1 cup fresh or frozen mixed berries (blueberries, raspberries, strawberries)

1 cup fresh spinach (lightly packed)

1/2 cup unsweetened almond milk or coconut water

1 tablespoon ground flaxseed or chia seeds

1–2 teaspoons pure maple syrup or raw honey

1/2 teaspoon vanilla extract

1. Preheat oven to 350°F (175°C) and lightly grease or line an 8x8-inch baking pan with parchment paper.

2. In a mixing bowl, whisk together almond flour, cocoa powder, baking soda, and salt.

3. In a separate bowl, whisk eggs, maple syrup (or date puree), oil, and vanilla until smooth.

4. Combine wet and dry ingredients until just mixed. Fold in chocolate chips or walnuts if using.

5. Pour batter into prepared pan and spread evenly.

6. Bake for 25–30 minutes, or until a toothpick comes out mostly clean (a few moist crumbs are okay).

7. Let cool completely in the pan before cutting into squares.

Optional Boost: Dust with a bit of cinnamon or serve with a dollop of unsweetened coconut yogurt.

Poached Pears with Ginger and Lemon

Prep Time: 10 minutes

Cook Time: 20–25 minutes

Servings: 2

Ingredients:

2 ripe but firm pears, peeled, halved, and cored

2 cups water

1 tablespoon freshly grated ginger or 1-inch knob, sliced

Zest and juice of 1 lemon

1–2 teaspoons raw honey or pure maple syrup

1/2 teaspoon ground cinnamon

Fresh mint for garnish

1. In a medium saucepan, combine water, ginger, lemon zest, lemon juice, and honey (if using). Bring to a gentle simmer.

2. Add pear halves to the pot, cut side down.

3. Cover and simmer for 20–25 minutes, turning pears halfway through, until they are tender but still hold their shape.

4. Remove pears from the liquid and set aside.

5. Optional: Simmer the poaching liquid uncovered for 5–10 more minutes to reduce into a light syrup.

6. Serve the pears warm or chilled, drizzled with a little of the poaching syrup and garnished with mint.

Optional Boost: Sprinkle with chopped walnuts or a pinch of turmeric before serving

Baked Pumpkin Squares with Oats and Spices

Prep Time: 10 minutes

Cook Time: 25–30 minutes

Servings: 9 squares

Ingredients:

1 cup pumpkin purée (unsweetened)

1 1/2 cups rolled oats (gluten-free if needed)

1/4 cup almond butter or unsweetened applesauce

1/4 cup pure maple syrup or honey

2 eggs or flax eggs for vegan version: 2 tbsp ground flax + 5 tbsp water

1/2 teaspoon baking powder

1 teaspoon ground cinnamon

1/2 teaspoon ground nutmeg

1/4 teaspoon ground ginger

1/4 teaspoon sea salt

1 teaspoon vanilla extract

Optional: 1/4 cup chopped walnuts or pumpkin seeds

1. Preheat oven to 350°F (175°C). Grease or line an 8x8-inch baking dish with parchment paper.

2. In a large bowl, whisk together pumpkin purée, eggs (or flax eggs), almond butter, maple syrup, and vanilla.

3. Add oats, baking powder, cinnamon, nutmeg, ginger, and salt. Stir until well combined.

4. Pour mixture into the prepared baking dish and spread evenly.

5. Top with chopped walnuts or pumpkin seeds if using.

6. Bake for 25–30 minutes or until the center is set and a toothpick comes out clean.

7. Let cool before slicing into squares.

Optional Boost: Serve with a dollop of plain Greek yogurt or drizzle of almond butter.

Date and Nut Energy Bites

Prep Time: 10–15 minutes

Servings: Makes about 12–14 bites

Ingredients:

1 cup Medjool dates (pitted)

1/2 cup raw almonds or walnuts

1/4 cup raw sunflower or pumpkin seeds

2 tablespoons ground flaxseed or chia seeds

1 tablespoon almond butter or tahini

1/2 teaspoon ground cinnamon

1/2 teaspoon vanilla extract (optional)

Pinch of sea salt

1–2 tablespoons water, if needed for blending

1. Add all ingredients to a food processor.

2. Pulse until the mixture is crumbly but sticky enough to hold together. Add a little water if it's too dry.

3. Scoop out about 1 tablespoon of mixture at a time and roll into balls using your hands.

4. Store in an airtight container in the fridge for up to 1 week, or freeze for up to 1 month.

Optional Boost: Roll the bites in unsweetened shredded coconut, hemp seeds, or cocoa powder for added nutrients and variety.

ANDREA D. RATLIFF

Beverages

Golden Turmeric Latte (Dairy-Free)

Prep Time: 5 minutes

Cook Time: 5 minutes

Servings: 1

Ingredients:

1 cup unsweetened almond milk or oat milk

1/2 teaspoon ground turmeric

Pinch of black pepper (essential for curcumin absorption)

1/4 teaspoon ground cinnamon

1/4 teaspoon ground ginger

1–2 teaspoons raw honey or pure maple syrup

1/4 teaspoon vanilla extract

1. In a small saucepan, combine almond milk, turmeric, black pepper, cinnamon, and ginger.

2. Heat gently over medium-low heat, whisking frequently, until hot but not boiling (about 3–5 minutes).

3. Remove from heat and stir in honey (or maple syrup) and vanilla, if using.

4. Pour into a mug. For a frothy version, use a milk frother or blend carefully for 10–15 seconds.

5. Sprinkle a little extra cinnamon on top if desired, and enjoy warm.

Optional Boost: Add a scoop of collagen peptides or dairy-free protein powder.

Green Tea or Matcha

Prep Time: 2–3 minutes

Cook Time: 5 minutes

Servings: 1

Option 1: Classic Green Tea

1 green tea bag or 1 teaspoon loose-leaf green tea

1 cup hot water (not boiling; around 175°F or 80°C)

Optional: squeeze of lemon, drizzle of raw honey

Instructions:

1. Heat water to just before boiling.

2. Steep the green tea bag or loose-leaf tea for 2–3 minutes.

3. Remove the tea bag or strain the leaves.

4. Add lemon and honey if desired. Sip slowly and enjoy.

Option 2: Matcha Tea (Whisked)

1 teaspoon matcha powder (culinary or ceremonial grade)

2 ounces hot water (not boiling)

6 ounces warm water or unsweetened almond milk (for a matcha latte)

Optional: 1/2 teaspoon honey or maple syrup, pinch of cinnamon

Instructions:

1. Sift matcha powder into a cup or bowl to remove clumps.

2. Add 2 oz hot water and whisk briskly in a zig-zag motion until frothy (use a bamboo whisk or milk frother).

3. Add the remaining warm water or steamed almond milk and stir.

4. Sweeten if desired and enjoy warm.

Optional Boost: Add turmeric and a crack of black pepper for a matcha golden latte.

Ginger-Lemon Herbal Tea

Prep Time: 5 minutes

Cook Time: 10 minutes

Servings: 2 cups

Ingredients:

2 cups water

1-inch piece of fresh ginger root, peeled and thinly sliced

Juice of half a lemon

1–2 teaspoons raw honey or pure maple syrup (optional)

Optional: pinch of ground turmeric or black pepper

1. In a small saucepan, bring water and sliced ginger to a boil.
2. Reduce heat and let it simmer for 10 minutes.
3. Remove from heat and strain the tea into two mugs.
4. Stir in fresh lemon juice and honey (if using).
5. Add turmeric or black pepper if desired, and serve warm.

Optional Boost: Add a sprig of fresh mint or a cinnamon stick.

Berry and Basil Infused Water

Prep Time: 5 minutes

Infusion Time: 1–4 hours (for best flavor)

Servings: 4 (makes about 4 cups)

Ingredients:

4 cups filtered water

1/2 cup mixed fresh berries (blueberries, strawberries, raspberries)

6–8 fresh basil leaves

Optional: juice of 1/2 lemon or a few lemon slices

1. Lightly crush the berries with the back of a spoon to release their juices.

2. Add crushed berries and basil leaves to a large pitcher or glass jar.

3. Pour in the filtered water and stir gently.

4. Let the mixture infuse in the refrigerator for at least 1 hour (up to 4 hours for more flavor).

5. Strain before serving if desired, or pour as-is over ice.

Optional Boost: Add cucumber slices or a few mint leaves.

Unsweetened Tart Cherry Juice (Diluted)

Prep Time: 2 minutes

Servings: 1

Ingredients:

1/2 cup unsweetened tart cherry juice (look for 100% juice with no added sugar)

1/2 to 1 cup filtered water

Ice (optional)

Lemon wedge or mint leaves

1. Pour tart cherry juice into a glass.

2. Add filtered water to dilute (start with 1/2 cup and adjust to your preferred strength).

3. Stir well. Add ice if desired.

4. Garnish with a lemon wedge or mint for a refreshing twist.

5. Serve.

Serving Tip: Limit to 1 small glass (about 4–6 oz total) per day to avoid excess natural sugars.

Cucumber Mint Spa Water

Prep Time: 5 minutes

Infusion Time: 1–2 hours (for best flavor)

Servings: 4 (about 4 cups)

Ingredients:

1/2 cucumber, thinly sliced

6–8 fresh mint leaves, gently bruised

4 cups filtered water

Ice (optional)

Lemon slices

1. In a large pitcher, combine cucumber slices and mint leaves.
2. Pour in the filtered water.
3. Optional: Add a few slices of lemon for a zesty twist.
4. Refrigerate for at least 1 hour to allow the flavors to infuse (up to 12 hours for a stronger taste).
5. Serve chilled over ice.

Optional Boost: Add a few slices of fresh ginger.

Hibiscus Iced Tea

Prep Time: 5 minutes

Steep Time: 15–20 minutes

Cooling Time: 30 minutes

Servings: 4 (about 1 cup each)

Ingredients:

4 cups water

1/4 cup dried hibiscus petals or 4 hibiscus tea bags

1–2 teaspoons raw honey or pure maple syrup (optional)

Fresh lemon or lime slices

Fresh mint leaves

1. Bring 4 cups of water to a boil.
2. Remove from heat and add dried hibiscus petals or tea bags.
3. Cover and steep for 15–20 minutes.
4. Strain out petals or remove tea bags.
5. Let cool, then refrigerate until chilled (about 30 minutes).
6. Pour over ice to serve. Add lemon or lime slices and fresh mint if desired.
7. Sweeten lightly with honey or maple syrup, if needed.

Optional Boost: Add a cinnamon stick while steeping.

Flaxseed Smoothie with Berries and Greens

Prep Time: 5 minutes

Servings: 2

Ingredients:

1 tablespoon ground flaxseed

1 cup frozen mixed berries

1 cup fresh spinach or kale (stems removed)

1 banana (for natural sweetness and creaminess)

1 cup unsweetened almond milk

1/2 teaspoon cinnamon

1–2 teaspoons pure maple syrup or raw honey (optional)

2–3 ice cubes

1. Add all ingredients to a blender.

2. Blend on high speed until smooth and creamy (about 30–60 seconds).

3. Taste and adjust sweetness as needed.

4. Pour into glasses and serve.

Optional Boost: Add a tablespoon of chia seeds or a scoop of plain Greek yogurt

Cinnamon-Spiced Almond Milk

Prep Time: 2 minutes

Cook Time: 5 minutes

Servings: 1

Ingredients:

1 cup unsweetened almond milk

1/2 teaspoon ground cinnamon

1/4 teaspoon ground ginger

1/4 teaspoon pure vanilla extract (optional)

1 teaspoon raw honey or pure maple syrup (optional)

Pinch of black pepper

1. In a small saucepan, heat almond milk over medium-low heat until warm but not boiling.

2. Stir in cinnamon, and optionally ginger, vanilla, and black pepper.

3. Whisk or froth until well combined and lightly steaming.

4. Pour into a mug and sweeten with honey or maple syrup if desired.

5. Sip slowly and enjoy as a relaxing bedtime ritual.

Optional Boost: Blend before serving for a creamier, latte-like texture, or top with a dusting of cinnamon.

Lemon Water with Apple Cider Vinegar (ACV)

Prep Time: 2 minutes

Servings: 1

Ingredients:

1 cup (8 oz) warm or room-temperature filtered water

1 tablespoon raw, unfiltered apple cider vinegar (with the "mother")

1 tablespoon fresh lemon juice

Optional:

1 teaspoon raw honey or a pinch of cinnamon

Thin slice of fresh ginger or turmeric root

1. In a glass, combine the water, lemon juice, and ACV.

2. Stir well to mix.

3. Add honey, cinnamon, or ginger if desired.

4. Drink slowly, preferably first thing in the morning or 15–30 minutes before meals.

Tips for Use:

Always rinse your mouth with water afterward or drink through a straw to protect tooth enamel.

Avoid taking undiluted ACV, which can irritate the throat or stomach lining.

Sauces, Dips, and Condiments

Classic Hummus

Prep Time: 10 minute

Servings: 4 (about 1/2 cup per serving)

Ingredients:

1 can (15 oz) chickpeas, drained and rinsed or 1.5 cups cooked

1/4 cup tahini

2 tablespoons fresh lemon juice (about 1 lemon)

1–2 cloves garlic, minced

2 tablespoons extra virgin olive oil (plus more for serving)

2–4 tablespoons water

1/2 teaspoon ground cumin

Sea salt, to taste

Paprika or chopped parsley

1. Add chickpeas, tahini, lemon juice, garlic, olive oil, and cumin (if using) to a food processor or blender.

2. Blend until smooth, adding water 1 tablespoon at a time until the hummus reaches your desired consistency.

3. Taste and adjust seasoning with salt or more lemon juice.

4. Transfer to a serving bowl. Drizzle with olive oil and garnish with paprika or fresh parsley if desired.

5. Serve with sliced cucumbers, bell peppers, carrot sticks, or whole grain pita.

Optional Boost: Add a pinch of turmeric or blend in roasted red peppers.

Avocado Cilantro Lime Sauce

Prep Time: 5–10 minutes

Servings: Makes about 1 cup (4–6 servings as a condiment or dip)

Ingredients:

1 ripe avocado

1/2 cup fresh cilantro leaves (lightly packed)

1 clove garlic

Juice of 1 lime (about 2 tablespoons)

2–3 tablespoons water (to thin)

1 tablespoon extra-virgin olive oil

Sea salt, to taste

Optional: pinch of ground cumin or a slice of jalapeño for a spicy kick

1. Add all ingredients to a blender or food processor.

2. Blend until smooth and creamy, scraping down the sides as needed.

3. Add more water, 1 tablespoon at a time, to reach your desired consistency.

4. Taste and adjust seasoning if needed.

5. Use or refrigerate in an airtight container for up to 2 days (place plastic wrap directly on the surface to minimize browning).

Serving Ideas: Use as a sauce for roasted vegetables, a topping for grain bowls, a dip for raw veggies, or a spread for wraps and sandwiches.

Basil Pesto (Dairy-Free)

Prep Time: 10 minutes

Servings: Makes about 3/4 cup (serves 4 as a topping)

Ingredients:

2 cups fresh basil leaves, packed

1/3 cup raw walnuts or pine nuts

2 garlic cloves

1/3 cup extra virgin olive oil

Juice of 1/2 lemon

Sea salt, to taste

Optional: 2 tablespoons nutritional yeast

1. In a food processor or high-speed blender, pulse the nuts and garlic until finely chopped.

2. Add basil, lemon juice, and salt. Pulse a few times to combine.

3. With the motor running, slowly drizzle in olive oil until the mixture is smooth and creamy. Scrape down sides as needed.

4. If using, blend in nutritional yeast for a savory, cheese-like flavor.

5. Taste and adjust seasoning. Add a splash more lemon juice or oil if desired.

6. Use or store in an airtight container in the fridge for up to 5 days.

Serving Suggestions:

Toss with roasted veggies or whole grain pasta

Spread on avocado toast

Drizzle over grilled fish or chicken

Swirl into soup or quinoa bowls

Miso-Ginger Sauce

Prep Time: 5 minutes

Servings: Makes about 1/2 cup (enough for 2–4 servings as a dressing or drizzle)

Ingredients:

2 tablespoons white or yellow miso paste (look for unpasteurized if possible, for live cultures)

1 tablespoon freshly grated ginger

1 tablespoon rice vinegar or apple cider vinegar

1 teaspoon toasted sesame oil

1 tablespoon water (more as needed to thin)

1 teaspoon pure maple syrup or raw honey

1 clove garlic, minced

A pinch of ground black pepper

1. In a small bowl or jar, whisk together miso paste, grated ginger, vinegar, sesame oil, and water.

2. Add maple syrup or honey if desired to balance the flavors.

3. Stir until smooth. Adjust consistency with additional water if needed.

4. Taste and adjust seasoning. Add garlic or black pepper if using.

5. Use or store in the fridge in an airtight container for up to 5 days.

Serving Ideas:

Drizzle over roasted veggies, grain bowls, or steamed greens.

Use as a dressing for salads or a dip for raw veggies.

Spoon over grilled tofu, salmon, or chicken for a savory kick.

Spicy Cashew Cream

Prep Time: 5 minutes (plus soaking time)

Servings: Makes about 1 cup (4–6 servings as a dip or sauce)

Ingredients:

1 cup raw cashews (soaked in water for at least 2 hours or overnight)

1/3 cup filtered water

1 garlic clove

2 tablespoons fresh lemon juice

1/4 teaspoon cayenne pepper

1/4 teaspoon sea salt

Optional: 1 tablespoon nutritional yeast for a cheesy flavor

1. Drain and rinse the soaked cashews.

2. Add cashews, water, garlic, lemon juice, cayenne, and salt to a high-speed blender or food processor.

3. Blend until smooth and creamy, scraping down sides as needed. Add more water a tablespoon at a time for a thinner consistency.

4. Taste and adjust seasoning as desired.

5. Store in an airtight container in the fridge for up to 5 days.

Serving Ideas: Use as a dip for raw veggies, a drizzle for grain bowls, a spread for wraps, or a creamy salad dressing base.

Cucumber-Dill Yogurt Sauce (Dairy-Free or Greek Yogurt)

Prep Time: 10 minutes

Servings: 4 (as a condiment or side)

Ingredients:

1 cup plain Greek yogurt or unsweetened dairy-free yogurt (such as coconut or almond-based, with live cultures)

1/2 cup finely grated cucumber (squeeze out excess water)

1 tablespoon fresh dill, finely chopped or 1 teaspoon dried dill

1 small garlic clove, minced

1 tablespoon fresh lemon juice

1 tablespoon extra-virgin olive oil

Sea salt and freshly ground black pepper, to taste

1. In a medium bowl, combine yogurt, grated cucumber, dill, garlic, lemon juice, and olive oil (if using).

2. Stir well to mix.

3. Season with salt and pepper to taste.

4. Chill in the refrigerator for at least 15 minutes to let the flavors meld.

5. Serve with grilled veggies, fish, or use as a dip or dressing.

Optional Boost: Add a pinch of ground cumin or chopped mint.

Apple Cider Vinaigrette

Prep Time: 5 minutes

Servings: Makes about 1/2 cup (serves 4–6)

Ingredients:

1/4 cup raw, unfiltered apple cider vinegar (with the "mother")

1/2 teaspoon Dijon mustard

1 teaspoon raw honey or pure maple syrup

1 clove garlic, finely minced or grated

1/3 cup extra virgin olive oil

Sea salt and freshly ground black pepper, to taste

1. In a small bowl or jar, whisk together the apple cider vinegar, Dijon mustard, honey (if using), and garlic.

2. Slowly drizzle in the olive oil while whisking continuously until the dressing is emulsified.

3. Season with salt and pepper to taste.

4. Store in a sealed jar in the fridge for up to 5 days. Shake well before using.

Serving Suggestions: Drizzle over mixed greens, roasted vegetables, or grain bowls

Chimichurri

Prep Time: 10 minutes

Servings: Makes about 3/4 cup (serves 4–6 as a condiment)

Ingredients:

1 cup fresh flat-leaf parsley, finely chopped

2 tablespoons fresh oregano or 2 teaspoons dried

3–4 cloves garlic, minced

1/2 cup extra virgin olive oil

2 tablespoons red wine vinegar or apple cider vinegar

1/4 teaspoon sea salt or to taste

1/4 teaspoon freshly ground black pepper

Optional: pinch of red pepper flakes for mild heat

Optional boost: squeeze of lemon juice

1. In a bowl, whisk together olive oil, vinegar, garlic, salt, pepper, and red pepper flakes (if using).

2. Stir in chopped parsley and oregano until well combined.

3. Let sit for at least 10 minutes to allow flavors to meld (can be made ahead and refrigerated).

4. Serve over grilled vegetables, roasted sweet potatoes, whole grain bowls, or lean proteins.

Storage: Keeps in an airtight container in the fridge for 3–4 days. Bring to room temperature before serving for best flavor.

ANDREA D. RATLIFF

SYMPTOMS/FLARE UP JOURNAL

WEEK 1

DATE	INGREDIENTS ELIMINATED	SYMPTOMS

WEEK 2

DATE	INGREDIENTS ELIMINATED	SYMPTOMS

WEEK 3

DATE	INGREDIENTS ELIMINATED	SYMPTOMS

WEEK 4

DATE	INGREDIENTS ELIMINATED	SYMPTOMS

Recipe Index

A
* Almond Flour Brownies (Naturally Sweetened) – p.114
* Apple Cider Vinaigrette – p.136
* Apple Slices with Almond Butter – p.98
* Avocado and Citrus Spinach Salad – p.55
* Avocado Chocolate Mousse – p.111
* Avocado Cilantro Lime Dressing – p.64
* Avocado Cilantro Lime Sauce – p.131
* Avocado on Whole Grain or Gluten-Free Crackers – p.102
* Avocado Toast on Whole Grain Bread – p.24

B
* Baked Apples with Walnuts and Maple Syrup – p.110
* Baked Pumpkin Squares with Oats and Spices – p.116
* Baked Salmon with Lemon and Dill – p.67
* Baked Tofu with Sweet Potato and Broccoli – p.77
* Banana Nice Cream – p.112
* Basil Pesto (Dairy-Free) – p.132
* Berry and Basil Infused Water – p.122
* Broccoli and Cauliflower Crunch Salad – p.60
* Brown Rice Sushi Rolls with Veggies and Avocado – p.40

C
* Cabbage and Apple Slaw with Almonds – p.57
* Chickpea and Kale Stir-Fry with Olive Oil and Garlic – p.37
* Chickpea and Spinach Coconut Curry – p.68
* Chia Pudding with Cinnamon and Berries – p.100
* Chia Pudding with Coconut Milk and Raspberries – p.29
* Chia Seed Pudding with Berries and Cinnamon – p.109
* Chimichurri – p.137
* Classic Hummus – p.130
* Coconut Yogurt Parfait with Almonds and Blueberries – p.113
* Cucumber and Avocado Salad – p.90
* Cucumber-Dill Yogurt Sauce (Dairy-Free or Greek Yogurt) – p.135
* Cucumber Mint Spa Water – p.124
* Curried Sweet Potato and Carrot Soup – p.48

D
* Dark Chocolate-Dipped Strawberries – p.108
* Date and Nut Energy Bites – p.117

ANDREA D. RATLIFF

E
- Edamame with a Dash of Sea Salt – p.105
- Eggplant and Mushroom Stir-Fry over Brown Rice – p.76

F
- Farro Bowl with Roasted Veggies and Lemon-Herb Dressing – p.79
- Flaxseed Smoothie with Berries and Greens – p.126
- Fresh Berries with a Handful of Walnuts – p.97

G
- Garlic Sautéed Spinach – p.87
- Ginger-Lemon Herbal Tea – p.121
- Golden Turmeric Latte (Dairy-Free) – p.119
- Greek Yogurt with Chia Seeds and Strawberries – p.23
- Greek Yogurt with Turmeric and Honey (or Cinnamon) – p.103
- Grilled Chicken and Sweet Potato Bowl – p.39
- Grilled Chicken with Quinoa and Roasted Broccoli – p.69
- Grilled Mackerel with Avocado Slaw – p.73
- Grilled Salmon Salad with Mixed Greens – p.56
- Grilled Salmon Salad with Olive Oil Vinaigrette – p.3
- Grilled Zucchini with Fresh Herbs – p.95

H
- Handful of Pumpkin Seeds or Sunflower Seeds – p.101
- Hearty Vegetable and Quinoa Stew – p.45
- Hibiscus Iced Tea – p.125
- Hummus with Carrot and Cucumber Sticks – p.99

L
- Lemon-Tahini Dressing – p.61
- Lemon Water with Apple Cider Vinegar (ACV) – p.12
- Lentil and Vegetable Soup with Turmeric – p.34

M
- Mashed Sweet Potatoes with Olive Oil – p.92
- Mediterranean Baked Cod with Tomatoes and Olives – p.84
- Mediterranean Chickpea Stew – p.50
- Mediterranean Hummus Plate – p.38
- Miso-Ginger Dressing – p.6
- Miso-Ginger Sauce – p.13
- Miso Soup with Tofu and Seaweed – p.46
- Miso-Glazed Cod with Steamed Greens and Brown Rice – p.80
- Moroccan-Spiced Chicken Thighs with Roasted Carrots – p.7

* Mushroom and Spinach Whole Grain Wrap – p.41

O
* Oatmeal with Berries and Walnuts – p.22
* Olive Oil & Apple Cider Vinaigrette – p.62

P
* Poached Pears with Ginger and Lemon – p.115

Q
* Quinoa Bowl with Roasted Veggies and Tahini Dressing – p.35
* Quinoa Porridge with Almond Butter and Sliced Apples – p.28
* Quinoa with Lemon and Parsley – p.88
* Quinoa and Vegetable-Stuffed Portobello Mushrooms – p.81

R
* Red Cabbage Slaw with Apple Cider Vinaigrette – p.93
* Roasted Brussels Sprouts with Balsamic Glaze – p.86
* Roasted Carrots with Cumin and Coriander – p.91
* Roasted Cauliflower Steaks with Herb Sauce – p.83
* Roasted Chickpeas with Sea Salt and Paprika – p.104

S
* Sardine and Avocado Wrap (Whole Grain or Lettuce Wrap) – p.36
* Scrambled Eggs with Turmeric and Veggies – p.26
* Smoothie Pops (Banana, Berries, and Spinach) – p.106
* Smoothie with Spinach, Blueberries, Banana, and Flaxseeds – p.25
* Spiced Red Lentil and Spinach Stew – p.53
* Spicy Cashew Cream – p.134
* Steamed Broccoli with Lemon and Pumpkin Seeds – p.94
* Stuffed Bell Peppers with Lentils and Brown Rice – p.71
* Sweet Potato and Black Bean Tacos – p.70
* Sweet Potato Hash with Kale and Olive Oil – p.31

T
* Tomato and White Bean Stew with Rosemary – p.49
* Turmeric Cauliflower Rice – p.89
* Turmeric Chicken and Vegetable Skillet – p.75
* Turmeric Ginger Lentil Soup – p.44
* Turmeric-Ginger Dressing – p.63

W
* Warm Farro Salad with Broccoli, Peas, and Lemon-Tahini Dressing – p.42
* Warm Sweet Potato and Spinach Salad – p.58
* Wild Rice and Cranberry Salad – p.59

ANDREA D. RATLIFF

- Wild Rice and Mushroom Soup – p.52
- Wild-Caught Shrimp Stir-Fry with Bok Choy and Ginger – p.74

Z
- Zucchini Noodles with Pesto and Cherry Tomatoes – p.72

Printed in Great Britain
by Amazon

62660107R00087